Creative
Counterpart

Creative Counterpart

LINDA DILLOW

THOMAS NELSON PUBLISHERS
Nashville • Camden • New York

Published in Nashville, Tennessee, by Thomas Nelson,
Inc., and distributed in Canada by Lawson Falle, Ltd.,
Cambridge, Ontario.

Printed in the United States of America.

Unless otherwise noted, all Scripture quotations are from THE NEW KING
JAMES VERSION. Copyright © 1979, 1980, 1982, Thomas Nelson, Inc.,
Publishers.

Scripture quotations noted NIV are from The Holy Bible: New International
Version. Copyright © 1973, 1978, International Bible Society. Used by
permission of Zondervan Bible Publishers.

Scripture quotations noted AMPLIFIED are from The Amplified Bible: Old
Testament, copyright © 1962, 1964 by Zondervan Publishing House (used
by permission) and from The Amplified New Testament, copyright © 1954,
1958 by the Lockman Foundation (used by permission).

Scripture quotations noted NASB are from the New American Standard Bible,
© The Lockman Foundation 1960, 1962, 1963, 1968, 1971, 1972, 1973,
1975, 1977, and are used by permission.

Scripture quotations noted TLB are from The Living Bible (Wheaton, Illinois:
Tyndale House Publishers, 1971) and are used by permission.

Library of Congress Cataloging-in-Publication Data

Dillow, Linda.
  Creative counterpart.

  Bibliography: p.
    1. Wives—Religious life.   2. Wives—Conduct of life.
I. Title.
BV4527.D54   1986   248.8'435   86–21648
ISBN 0–8407–3067–5 (pbk.)

Contents

TO JODY,

MY BELOVED AND MY FRIEND,
WHOSE LOVE, ENCOURAGEMENT,
AND LOGICAL MIND
MADE THIS BOOK POSSIBLE

Foreword

A number of years have transpired since the first salvos were fired in the renewed crusade for women's rights. We have been jarred from our complacency (and that's good!) by spasms of ink-slinging feminists picking up their standards and marching in both directions. Like reincarnated phantoms of the French Revolution, shock troops waved the banner of *Liberté, Egalité, Fraternité*. Countercrusaders responded with a simplistic white flag on which was scrawled a single word: *Submission!*

Controversy continues, and Christian wives strain to focus in on the hearings. Should we be aligned with one side or the other? Do we fight what we find, or do we surrender to it? On what basis do we decide? Furthermore, what long-term guarantee is there against depreciation?

Many of our answers are at once profound and pitifully naive. We keep asking, "What does the Bible say?" When we find out what it says, we complain that it does not fit. So we try to form it to fit our preconceived notions. Using either highhanded "scholarship," which twists the text to say what we want it to say, or a clumsy simplification, which washes out to *reductio ad absurdum*, we run about mouthing fragments of "the gospel according to women."

Creative Counterpart is not a complete manual on womanhood, nor is it an exhaustive study of Christian marriage. It is a choice morsel, laced with practical fiber, for women who want to be wives in the simple manner of which the Scriptures speak, culture notwithstanding.

It has been my privilege to know Linda Dillow not only as a seminary student's wife but as a friend and a sister in the faith of our Lord Jesus Christ. I have observed her at home as well as on the public platform. She instills confidence in the observer. With a quiet strength that exudes the fragrance of the 1 Peter example of womanhood, she combines inner quiet beauty with an incredible toughness of conviction. Her refined style at the rostrum reflects her inner core of cheerful dedication and good-humored discipline.

Linda does not preach. She writes neither technically nor sarcastically, but her words are an intelligent and human application of what the Bible says to wives. Her portrait of marriage is drawn with well-defined strokes, which lift the role of wifehood to a level of dignity and significance.

The book has been born late in the line of apologetics for Christian marriages. Perhaps this timing allows both reader and writer an extra measure of relativity. At any rate, the one who ponders these pages will be refreshed with a cool breeze, a delightfully readable, and altogether profitable discussion of marriage and home-making.

Jeanne W. Hendricks
Dallas, Texas

The Honeymoon Disaster

The giant logging truck barreled toward us as we headed our heavily laden car up the winding road. Pulling sharply to the right, Jody missed the truck, but in the process our car landed in a ditch.

As I tried to regain my composure, the events of the past three days raced through my mind: the wedding and two glorious days in the cabin by the river. Such a rustic, yet romantic place—a huge fireplace, a balcony overhanging the rushing river and, best of all, being alone with my new husband.

I could have been content to stay forever at the Hawthorne Farms cottage on the river, but such luxuries were impossible for two newly married college students. Two nights were all our budget of two hundred dollars a month would allow. Thus, to prolong our honeymoon we had decided to camp.

Mistake number one! Neither Jody nor I knew anything about camping. Yet here we were, with a tent, sleeping bags, and supplies, sitting in a ditch! With Jody pushing and me steering we finally left the ditch. On the road again, we found a lovely, secluded campsite and struggled with the tent. Was this supposed to be fun?

Exhausted, we fell into our sleeping bags early, only

to be awakened at midnight by a gentle rain that became a torrential downpour. Being *bright* college students, we soon discovered our borrowed tent had a huge leak, and we were fast on our way to being soaked! Such a delightful way to spend the third night of our honeymoon—breaking camp and packing a sopping wet tent in a downpour at 1:00 A.M.! Romance at its height! But our problems had just begun. . . .

Driving down the mountain in the wee hours of the morning, we had a flat tire! I held the flashlight and umbrella while Jody changed the tire alongside the narrow road. He looked up at me, smiling, "Honey, I guess these are the kinds of things that bind you together in marriage!"

I look back now, twenty-two years and four children later, and realize that neither Jody nor I had any idea of the many joys, sorrows, and ridiculous circumstances that would bind us as one. I had no idea of all I had to learn about loving my husband. Nor was I aware of all the "nagging" abilities that lay dormant within me.

I married Jody because I wanted to be his friend, lover, and companion forever. I've never met a woman who married because she felt it would make her miserable! Each foresees fulfillment and satisfaction with her partner. As the years pass, however, something happens. Sometimes Prince Charming begins to turn into a toad or Cinderella turns into a nag, and the exciting relationship can become a daily drag.

Most often I have found that a woman who is dissatisfied with her marriage usually points to three reasons: (1) *Her husband,* "If he were just more affectionate, or more aggressive, or more helpful, or more anything, I could be the kind of wife I should be"; (2) *her circum-*

stances, "If I lived in a bigger house, or if I didn't have such a big house to clean; if I had a child, or if I *didn't* have so many children," and of course, "If we had more money, I could be a better wife"; (3) *herself,* "If I were just different—beautiful, thin, talented, successful, intelligent, creative, sexy—then I could be the wife of the year." And she may add, "But I'm me, and the daily drag will continue." That's where she's wrong!

As you read these pages you will discover creative suggestions to motivate your husband, to counsel you on how you can live *above* your circumstances, and to help you develop a plan whereby you can begin to become the woman, wife, and mother that you long to be!

2

The Beautiful Blueprint

"A woman has been the most influential person in my life," said 212 of the 250 persons contacted in a research survey.[1] Many of them named a wife or a mother, but teachers, grandmothers, and Sunday school workers also appeared on the list. We have all heard William R. Wallace's words: "the hand that rocks the cradle rules the world," but did you know that it was Abraham Lincoln who added, "And all that I am or hope to be I owe to my angel mother"?

We have been conditioned by today's advertising to respond instantly to the word *housewife* with the word *drudgery*. Here is a typical scene in a magazine ad: an exhausted woman dressed like Miss Rummage Sale 1956 is slouched over an ironing board with six small children and the family dog wrapped around her ankles, and a pot is boiling over on the stove. This is accompanied by a comforting message that after a grueling day in the home she can always take Excedrin to kill the pain, Nytol to calm her down, or Geritol to pep her up.

Partly as a result of this conditioning, a woman may begin to question herself, her role, and life in general. And many women are frustrated. One woman told me she could not wait until her four children were all in

14

school so she could go out and contribute something to society. Every day she longed for them to go to bed so she could do something constructive for someone.

Isn't there more to being a wife and mother than refolding towels that a husband folds wrong, keeping the static out of the family underwear, getting kids to Little League on time, and trying to keep peace in the midst of teenage chaos? I believe that there is much more, and the much more is exciting! Too many women have been brainwashed into thinking the life of a wife and mother consists entirely of the "three C's": *cooking, cleaning,* and *car-pooling.*

Yes, there are frustrated wives, just as there are frustrated engineers, airplane pilots, and karate instructors. But the frustration does not stem from the nature of the work; rather, it comes from the boredom inevitable in any job done poorly or unimaginatively.

A *creative counterpart* is more than just a helper. She is a woman who, having chosen (or having found herself in) the vocation of wife and mother, decides to learn and grow in all the areas of this role and to work as hard as if she were aiming for the presidency of a corporation.

Functioning as a professional in all areas of marriage is the essence of being a *creative counterpart*. Let's look at one such *creative counterpart* described many years ago in the book of Proverbs. There are many outstanding, godly women mentioned throughout the Bible, but this woman received special praise: "Many daughters have done well, / But you excel them all" (Prov. 31:29). Who was this woman who did more than Deborah, the military adviser, or Ruth, the woman of constancy, or Esther, the queen who risked her life for her people? She was a wife and mother like you and me!

A study of this proverb reveals that verses 10 through 31 are a description of the virtuous wife. This passage is designed to show a woman what kind of wife she should be and to show a man what kind of woman he should choose to marry. It is also an acrostic poem; each of the twenty-two verses begins with a letter of the Hebrew alphabet in successive order, making it a literary as well as a spiritual masterpiece.

We learn much about this wise wife as we view her character in these verses, yet we do not know her name. We are told not *who* she was but *what* she was. A godly character like hers is what each of us needs to become a *creative counterpart*. Let's look together at her inward character and then at her outward appearance.

INWARD CHARACTER

Gordon MacDonald has recently identified inward character as a person's private world, the command center that directs all activities. In the Bible this private world was often referred to as the heart. Proverb 4:23 says, "Keep your heart with all diligence, / For out of it spring the issues of life."

The condition of an individual's private world, says Gordon MacDonald, determines how well that individual will deal with crisis situations and everyday life.[2] Let's look at the inner world or heart of the woman in Proverb 31. You might want to read the entire portrait of this woman on page 17 before we begin.

THE WISE WOMAN OF PROVERB 31

Who can find a virtuous wife?
  For her worth is far above rubies.
The heart of her husband safely trusts her;
  So he will have no lack of gain.

She does him good and not evil
  All the days of her life.
She seeks wool and flax,
  And willingly works with her hands.

She is like the merchant ships,
  She brings her food from afar.
She also rises while it is yet night,
  And provides food for her household,
And a portion for her maidservants.

She considers a field and buys it;
  From her profits she plants a vineyard.
She girds herself with strength,
  And strengthens her arms.

She perceives that her merchandise is good,
  And her lamp does not go out by night.
She stretches out her hands to the distaff,
  And her hand holds the spindle.

She extends her hand to the poor,
  Yes, she reaches out her hands to the needy.
She is not afraid of snow for her household,
  For all her household is clothed with scarlet.
  She makes tapestry for herself;
  Her clothing is fine linen and purple.

Her husband is known in the gates,
  When he sits among the elders of the land.
She makes linen garments and sells them,
  And supplies sashes for the merchants.

Strength and honor are her clothing;
  She shall rejoice in time to come.
She opens her mouth with wisdom,
  And on her tongue is the law of kindness.

She watches over the ways of her household,
  And does not eat the bread of idleness.
Her children rise up and call her blessed;
  Her husband also, and he praises her:
"Many daughters have done well,
  But you excel them all."

Charm is deceitful and beauty is vain,
  But a woman who fears the LORD, she shall be praised.
Give her of the fruit of her hands,
  And let her own works praise her in the gates.

(10–31)

TRUSTWORTHY

First, she was trustworthy.

In the New American Standard version of the Bible this passage begins with the question: "An excellent wife, who can find?" The word *excellent* means "a woman of strength."[3] It is the same word used to describe the character of Israel's judges, indicating that they were able and well qualified for their profession. So it follows that a wise woman is able and qualified for her work, has command of her own spirit, and is able to manage others. She is a woman of resolution who, having chosen godly principles, is firm and faithful to them.[4] "Who can find a virtuous wife?" indicates that such a woman is very rare and can't be found on every block in middle America.

Trust was very important to our friend in Proverbs

31, and it is necessary to every marriage. The husband of this kind of wife has reason to trust her conduct (her behavior in company) because of the way she has treated him in past years. He knows she will always be loyal and never betray him.

Several years ago when Jody and I were working in a campus ministry, I was gathering material for teaching girls about the Christian view of sex, love, and marriage. I asked Jody what he appreciated most in me as a wife, and in his logical way he replied, "Your faithfulness."

Faithfulness? I thought. *How dull!* I could think of many more exciting attributes for him to mention.

I'm sure my disappointment expressed itself in a slight frown, because he went on to explain, "The most important thing to a man is to know that the woman he loves is on his team. If the rest of the world calls him a fool and deserts him, she'll be there beside him."

A strong bond of faithfulness and trust must have existed between the woman in Proverb 31 and her husband. Some commentators have said that this trust could also be applied to her husband's confidence in her ability to manage the household affairs: he knew that she was competent and that when he returned from his work each evening, he would find the home and family not in chaos but in order. Which of these situations does your husband find when he walks in the door?

This trustworthy woman would never do anything to bring dishonor to her husband's name. She would not confide to her best friend how he had hurt her or get a laugh at the bridge table by listing his faults. Her own conduct was above reproach. We read, "She does him good and not evil / All the days of her life."

Note that this commitment was not for a month or

a year but for all the days of her life. Such a statement indicated a decision of her will (not an emotion) to stand by his side forever, regardless of what happened to them. Today it seems common to love your husband and do him good until problems come (he loses his job or his business goes bad or your teenager is tempted by alcohol or drugs); then it's every person for himself or herself!

"You live your life and I'll live mine. You do your thing and I'll do mine. As long as they mesh, it's beautiful, but as soon as they grate, we'll split!" In contrast, 1 Corinthians 13:7 says that love endures all things. The model wife of Proverb 31 made a commitment to do good, to truly love her husband all the days of her life.

This woman's beliefs were lived out in the relationship between her and her husband. She exemplified the apostle Paul's words to the Corinthians, "We do all things, beloved, for your edification [building them up and helping them grow in Christ]" (2 Cor. 12:19). When the wise wife applied this to her husband, she treated him with this attitude: "I will do everything, my beloved, for your benefit." She considered every word and action and then said and did only what would build him up and help him. The virtuous wife was *trustworthy*, and she was also *industrious*.

INDUSTRIOUS

Many activities in a woman's world (as well as in a man's world) are not superexciting! Maybe the housewife on TV is ecstatic because Lysol Basin Tub & Tile Cleaner gets her bathroom sparkling clean or because Mop 'n Glo makes her tingly all over, but somehow these products don't give me the same overjoyed feeling! In fact, I don't even remotely like cleaning the bathtub.

Yet this passage says the wise woman "willingly works with her hands." God doesn't say we have to be overjoyed; He says we are to do everything willingly. We are to have a positive attitude because we are doing this job for the people God has given us to love.

Are you willing to work hard, or do you look for excuses to avoid unpleasant tasks? I have a friend who is very depressed and unhappy. I truly believe one of the main causes of her depression is that she will not do anything that takes work. This verse tells us it is our attitude that counts, not whether we sew designer clothes or cook gourmet meals.

The virtuous wife's industrious spirit was also evident in her vigilance: "She watches over the ways of her household, / And does not eat the bread of idleness."

Oh, how I love to be idle! Give me a good book, a diet drink, and a bowl of popcorn, and I'm tempted to let the house and the people who dwell in it fend for themselves. Some women are industrious by nature, but most of us can identify with the honest wife who said, "I am a weak, lazy, and indifferent character, casual when I should be concerned, concerned when I should be carefree. I am often self-indulgent and hypocritical, begging God to help me when I am hardly willing to lift a finger for myself."

I am an industrious cook because I like to cook; I enjoy spending time preparing a week's meals to put in the freezer. I am not industrious about cleaning out closets and drawers because I loathe it. I will never forget one nightmare in which I watched with embarrassment as my friends went through my drawers after my funeral. How upset I was that they saw the state of disarray! This dream turned my idleness into activity, and I spent the next day industriously cleaning drawers and closets.

The wise wife had a trustworthy and industrious spirit. Third, she was organized.

ORGANIZED

In Solomon's time, the wife got up before the others in her household to start preparing and cooking the day's food and to plan the tasks to assign to her maids. The wise woman of Proverb 31 "rises while it is yet night, / And provides food for her household, / And a portion for her maidservants."

I believe that the virtuous wife was also up early for another reason: to prepare herself spiritually as well as physically for the day's demands. The Amplified Bible translates this passage: "She rises while yet it is night and gets spiritual food for her household." This wife knew that if she said a good morning to God first, her good mornings to everyone else would be better.

Jody and I had an inside joke about this verse. He would say, "Honey, when are you going to rise while it is still night like the virtuous wife?" And I would reply, "Whenever I see the maids coming in the door."

In the early years of our marriage, a day in the Dillow home began in one of two ways. The first was for me to sleep through the alarm, finally drag my tired body out of bed, throw on my robe, and rush into the girls' room to tell them to hurry or they would be late. Then I scurried into Tommy's room, encouraging my four-year-old son to dress quickly, and raced to the kitchen to do all the things I should have done the night before.

Finally, I threw breakfast on the table just in time for us to gulp down our food while I repeatedly encouraged everyone to hurry. By the end of breakfast everyone was bickering, and I was wondering why the family was so nervous and uptight!

The second way was for me to get up before my family, get dressed, and then sit on the couch as I talked to the Lord about the day ahead and gave whatever happened to Him. After spending time with Him, I walked into Joy and Robin's room, kissed them both, and awakened them cheerfully. I had plenty of time to awaken Tommy in the same loving manner.

Since the dishwasher was emptied, the lunches made, and the table set the night before, making breakfast was easy. Everyone had time to enjoy the morning meal and, as a result, was able to walk out the door with a smile. Of course some days fell in between these two extremes, but my family have said they much prefer the second way.

The virtuous wife was so well organized that she had spare time to be a businesswoman: "She considers a field and buys it; / From her profits she plants a vineyard." She also made linen garments and sold them.

The word *considers* stands out to me, since I occasionally have trouble saying the important word *no*. This prudent woman weighed each decision before assuming a new responsibility. Sometimes we are asked to become involved in many activities, and unless we know our priorities, we can easily become overextended. I am learning not to say yes immediately to every worthwhile activity, but instead to ask for time to think and pray about my decision.

Trustworthy, industrious, organized—these words

describe the woman of Proverb 31. One more word is needed to complete the picture of her character: *loving*.

LOVING

The virtuous wife was loving in her actions and in her words: "She opens her mouth with wisdom, / And on her tongue is the law of kindness."

The Amplified Bible translates this verse: "She opens her mouth with skillful and godly Wisdom." Here wisdom is equated with skill; this woman had skillful counsel and wise instruction for others.

Living life according to God's principles is truly a skill, even more complex than playing a violin or sewing an elegant evening gown. The wise woman of Proverbs 31 worked hard at developing this special skill, and it showed in the way she lived, in the words she spoke, and in the counsel she gave to others.

Just think for a minute what our homes and our world would be like if each of us applied this verse to our everyday lives. Would there be a difference in your relationship with your husband and children if you only opened your mouth with wisdom and if the law of kindness were on your tongue? Have you ever noticed a difference between the intonation you reserve for your friends and the one you use with your family? It's so easy to give our best to comparative strangers and toss our families the leftovers.

One young mother of eight children came into the family room and found all her children bickering. She gently admonished them, "Children, don't you know the Bible says we should be kind to one another?" Her eldest, who was nine, looked thoughtfully around the room and replied, "But, Mommy, there's nobody here but the family!"

The virtuous wife had so much love to give that it didn't stop with her family. Her hands were continually outstretched to anyone in need: "She extends her hand to the poor, / Yes, she reaches out her hands to the needy."

I remember speaking to a group of doctors' wives on the subject of the reality of Christianity in a woman's world. Afterward a smartly dressed woman approached me and said, "I think it's nice that you talk about a relationship with God, but what do you contribute to society? Do you ever go down into the ghetto to really help people?"

"God has given me a husband and small children," I replied, "and they come first in my life. Because of them I don't go to the ghetto, but I don't have to! There are so many needs in my neighborhood that I don't have to step one foot beyond it."

I've lived in many average American neighborhoods, and within a few square blocks there were always people who were divorced, separated, or together but fighting; children who had special problems; young mothers who were battling depression and bitterness; people who were sick—all people who were in need. How can anyone think the ghetto is the only place where people have problems?

I can contribute to society by remaining right where I am, and so can you. The key is first to put your hand in God's. Tell Him you're available and willing to give of yourself, and ask Him to show you where you can help. I'm certain He'll answer by opening your eyes to a situation in which you can stretch out your hands to someone who needs you.

Sometimes we hesitate to get involved because we know involvement means a commitment of time and love. It means extending ourselves as the woman in Proverb 31 did, and once we make a commitment to help, we are sometimes surprised at what God has for us. For example, He gave my family a 130-pound, 5-foot-4-inch son!

When we moved to Austria eight years ago, our son Tommy became good friends with Niki, a young boy in our neighborhood whose family had serious problems. During the next years Niki spent a great deal of time at our house and began going to church with us. He heard about the love of Christ in Sunday school, and Tommy and I had several talks with him about what it means to be a Christian. One day, sitting on the floor of Tommy's room, Niki prayed to receive Christ as his personal Savior.

As the tensions in his home increased, he spent more and more time in our home. We jokingly called him our Austrian son to show how fond we were of him. Yet, it was still a surprise when God brought Niki at age thirteen to live with us permanently. A surprise and a great joy!

Now I have four teenagers: Niki who is fourteen; Tom fifteen; Robin sixteen; and Joy eighteen. Four teenagers keep us broke, broken, and blessed, but how we thank God for His perfect plan.

These four adjectives—*trustworthy, industrious, organized,* and *loving*—characterized the spirit of the virtuous wife. The inner qualities led her to live a life that blessed others.

OUTWARD APPEARANCE

Very little was said about the virtuous woman's outward appearance, quite a contrast from the lengthy description of the bride in the Song of Solomon. Apparently this writer was so impressed with the wise woman's inner qualities and her outward actions that he did not notice her looks.

The writer did mention that her clothing was of fine linen and purple, but just a few lines later he noted that strength and honor were her real clothing. It seems that her inner qualities showed in her face and stature. She even carried herself with a regal bearing. How many millions of dollars do we women spend to look beautiful on the outside? True beauty comes from inner strength of character and cannot be bought or applied with expensive creams.

This description of the wise woman ended with the testimony of those who knew her best: her children and her husband. Her children blessed her for their early training as they grew up and went out into public life. "Many daughters have done well," said her husband. "But you excel them all." No one could give this woman greater compliments.

I could have plaques on my wall inscribed with flowery words of praise from the Chamber of Commerce, the Ladies Missionary Society, the PTA, the Girl Scouts, and my sorority alumnae group, but what would these mean in comparison with the praise of those who know me best? When people who live with me day in and day out say I have blessed them, it means something! Today as I sat writing about this woman, Jody came into the room and said, "Honey, you're a fantastic wife." Would ten thousand words from someone else have meant as much?

By now I'm sure you are thinking, *This woman was perfect! I could never be like her!* She was incredible, but God would not use her as the example of the "excellent wife" unless we, too, could grow to become like her.

As you look at the praise given to this woman and learn about her inward character, you should be encouraged to remember that she had grown children. Her inner qualities did not appear overnight but were hammered out in the trials of life as she trusted God and obeyed Him.

After giving us this long list of the woman's virtues and the testimonies of her family's praise, the writer ended by answering the important questions: How was the virtuous wife so perfect? How was she able to benefit her family, herself, and others?

The key to her success was that she feared the Lord. The writer said, "Charm is deceitful and beauty is vain, / But a woman who fears the LORD, she shall be praised."

A modern paraphrase might read, "Charm is often deceiving, hiding an ugly personality, and beauty is only skin deep, but a woman who fears God is truly charming and lovely." The virtuous wife first and foremost feared and worshiped God. She was trustworthy, industrious, organized, loving, and much more. The key to becoming like this wife, to becoming a *creative counterpart*, is to begin where she did, with a vital relationship with God.

Do you want to be like the wise wife? I do! And the starting place is the same for us, our relationship with God.

⊰ 3 ⊱

God's Game Plan

Through the centuries, women have read about the virtuous wife in Proverb 31 and wanted to be like her. Every wife would like to be described as trustworthy, industrious, organized, and loving. What wife wouldn't delight in being praised by her husband and children and told, "You're the best of all!"

We have spoken of how the virtuous wife worked hard to learn to live by God's principles, but we have also said that she was a product of God's working within her. So the question is raised, Who does it? If a woman wants to become a *creative counterpart*, will God do it through her or will she have to do it? Often a woman picks one or the other: either she sits and waits for God to make her a *creative counterpart*, or she sets up a program whereby she does all the work to become a virtuous wife.

I MUST DO IT ALL (or The Guilt Trip)

Susan is such a wife. Her overemphasis is on the part of the individual. She thinks people are responsible for their own spiritual progress, so she reads the commandments of Scripture and then sets up a program to obey them. After reading a book on marriage or attending a seminar, she does everything she can to live the principles. The problem is that she falls into a frustrating cycle. The harder she tries, the more she fails. The more she fails, the guiltier she feels. The guiltier she feels, the harder she tries. And round and round she goes, seemingly trapped in a life of frustration. She has reduced the New Testament to a set of rules or laws, and she does the same with the books she reads and the seminars she attends. Because she is unclear as to exactly how God will help her in the struggle, she is trapped in a cycle.

The New Testament exhortations to be a virtuous wife seem a dreadful burden. She views them as external laws to be obeyed. She constantly compares herself with other women who seem to better understand the job of being a wife. Her experience with the "law" is similar to that of the apostle Paul, "I do not understand what I do. For what I want to do I do not do, but what I hate I do" (Rom 7:15 NIV).

Susan's problem is complicated because her husband has severe emotional problems. He spends much of his time in deep depressions, and he takes his frustration out on her and the children. The more she tries to be what she is "supposed to be," the more she seems to be reminded of her failure. He spends money irresponsibly and bounces checks all over town, his lifestyle is immoral, and he is adversely affecting the children. All her attempts to love him are rebuffed with indifference and insensitivity. Emotionally she is drained, but she feels guilty because she is unable to respond as the woman who taught the seminar told her she should. Thus the guilt mounts.

GOD DOES IT ALL (or The Mystical Takeover)

Mary, on the other hand, thinks God will do it all. Her motto is, "Let go and let God!" She believes if she just trusts Jesus, the Holy Spirit will do all the work through her. God alone will remove her inconsistencies and automatically make her like the wife of Proverb 31.

She talks very spiritually and really sounds like a candidate for sainthood, but her husband can't stand to live with her. He is not a Christian and is highly offended by her "spiritual" tone. Her home is usually a mess, she is not a good wife, and her children are among the most undisciplined on the block. She is just "trusting Jesus" to take over and do the work through her. To all the world she sounds like a victorious Christian. She says all the right words and talks in glowing terms of how the Lord works through her in this or that circumstance.

Inside, however, Mary is miserable. She knows in her heart that her life does not match her glowing spiritual talk. She is inwardly frustrated because no matter how often she speaks of "God doing it through her," God doesn't seem to be doing much through her. She sincerely wants to be a better wife and mother, but her Christianity isn't producing the expected results. It has never dawned on her that part of the problem could be her view of the Christian life. The result is that while she sits waiting for God to work, she not only becomes frustrated and guilt-ridden, just like Susan, but she also has started spending large quantities of time and energy searching for the "secret" of the Spirit-filled life.

A young woman with Mary's perspective once told me she knew God did not want her to get up and have a devotional time in the morning because, as she explained, "I told God if He wanted me to get up and have a devotional time, then He could get me up at six-thirty, and I didn't wake up until seven-thirty." When I asked her if she had an alarm clock, she replied that she didn't do anything unless God motivated her. God did it all, and she was to do only what she felt He was motivating her to do.

THE BALANCE: 100 PERCENT + 100 PERCENT

Both Susan and Mary are sincere, both have good motives and desire to become like the Proverb 31 wife, but both are miserable and frustrated.

Paul put it all in focus: "You must be even more careful to do the good things that result from being saved, obeying God with deep reverence, shrinking back from all that might displease him. For God is at work within you, helping you want to obey him, and then helping you do what he wants" (Phil. 2:12–13 TLB).

Paul instructed the Philippians to do what God would want *because* of his unconditional love and forgiveness toward them. They were to obey, not wait for God to make them want to obey, because of what He did for them in giving them eternal and abundant life in Jesus. They were to do the positive and shrink back from the negative. And they would be able to do that because God would be constantly at work within them through the Holy Spirit, helping them want to obey and then helping them do all that God requires.

This is the balance. It's not 100 percent God or 100 percent me; neither is it 50 percent God and 50 percent me. It's 100 percent God *and* 100 percent me—both of us doing our 100 percent together. A relationship with God is much like a marriage relationship: each partner must give 100 percent.

GOD'S 100 PERCENT

In a marriage relationship there is the possibility that either partner can fail, hurt the other, decide to leave, or forsake the commitment. In a relationship with God only one partner can fail, hurt, or forsake, and I guarantee it's not God! Let's look at all He has already done for us and what He is doing for us every day.

NEW POSITION

"For He made Him who knew no sin to be sin for us, that we might become the righteousness of God in Him" (2 Cor. 5:21). We sinners have been declared righteous! We stand in grace; we are justified. If we know Jesus Christ as our personal Savior and Lord, there is nothing we can do to increase or decrease God's love for us.

If I were to read my Bible twelve hours and do twenty-nine good deeds today, God would not love me any more than He did before. (He would be *shocked* if I read my Bible for twelve hours, but it wouldn't increase His love for me!) We might interpret being justified as being just as if we had never sinned. God receives us not on the basis of how well we live up to the beautiful blueprint in Proverb 31 but completely on the merits of His Son.

Have you at times felt like a failure as a wife? I know I have! What a comfort to know God does not accept me on the basis of how well I succeed in doing what He wants me to do. Because of Christ's death, every barrier to full fellowship with God has been removed. I stand totally accepted, not on the basis of how I perform but on the basis of Christ's merits.

NEW PERSON

To *regenerate* is "to endow with new life and vigor," "to renew spiritually." This is exactly what Paul described in 2 Corinthians 5:17: "Therefore, if anyone is in Christ, he is a new creation; old things have passed away; behold, all things have become new."

God has given each of us a new nature, resulting in a new motivation toward godliness. This is proved by the very fact of your desire to understand what God wants you to understand about being His woman in the home. It is what Peter called desiring the pure milk of the Word (see 1 Pet. 2:2) and is characteristic of everyone who knows Christ personally. Thank God He has given you this desire! Those outside of Christ know of no such desire, which is one reason the national divorce rate is close to one out of every two marriages now. God has given you the desire to be the kind of *creative counterpart* that will enable you and your family to live the maximum life. Praise Him for what He has already done!

NEW POWER

How would you like "to be set apart as holy, to be consecrated"? Guess what? God has already promised this for you as He progressively makes you more like Himself. At the moment you received Jesus Christ as your Savior, God gave you the Holy Spirit, who will teach you the deep things of God, will guide you into all truth, and will give you power to live the Christian life. God knows no one could ever live it without His help.

God has done much for us in the past, yet it is easy to focus on our circumstances and to forget His faithfulness. Recently I was reading through Genesis and Exodus and was again overwhelmed at the marvelous miracles God performed for the Israelites. I read of the ten plagues He brought upon Egypt to convince Pharaoh to release the people, and then of the journey that brought them to the Red Sea.

Imagine being one of that company milling in panic beside the water, Pharaoh's army in hot pursuit. The only way you can escape death by the sword is death by drowning. Then, as the sun goes down, a strong wind sweeps in and parts the waters right before your eyes. A path becomes visible through the middle of the sea! A gasp from the people behind you causes you to whirl around to see a gigantic pillar of fire, which has appeared between you and the Egyptian chariots. All through the night the fiery glow illuminates the camp and the path that is drying on the seabed. On the other side of the pillar the Egyptians have been plunged into total darkness, and they await the morning light to renew their chase.

With the first rays of the dawn Moses gives the command. Hesitating for a moment between the towering walls of sea water on either side of the path and amid the clanks and cries and whines from the Egyptian camp, you move forward, down onto the now-solid seabed, and across to the other side. As the last of your people reach safety, your pursuers rush down onto the same path through the sea! Panic grips you again, but then you see Moses stretch out his hand over the sea. With a mighty roar, the walls of water come crashing down on the Egyptians! Their heavy armor and chariots pull them to the bottom, and the waters close over them. In a few moments, no trace of your enemies remains. God has delivered you! You'll never doubt God again after such a string of miracles!

Or will you? We humans forget so quickly. History tells us that just three days later the Israelites began to grumble to Moses because of their circumstances.

It's easy for us to think, *How* could *they?* But a look at our own lives shows us how quickly we forget all God has done for us. Think about what God has done in your marriage this year. Where have you seen His faithfulness to you as a wife? Too often we are just like the Israelites. We see only our present circumstances and fail to remember all God has done.

During difficult times in our marriage, I've made myself go away alone and write out a list of all God's faithfulnesses, of the growth in our marriage relationship, and of all I have to be thankful for. This exercise has helped me remember what God has done and get a better perspective about the present circumstances. We are continually exhorted through Scripture to remember what God has done. I'm convinced that if we do, it will make a tremendous difference in our lives. We need to remember that God has not only justified and regenerated us but has given us Himself as our companion. He has not left us alone to live the Christian life; He has actually come to live within us to empower each of us to be a *creative counterpart*.

NEW PROMISES

Now, how can this power be experienced in our lives? The answer to that leads us into a consideration of what God promises to do. Not only must we see what He has already done, but we must claim by faith what He promises to do.

HE'LL NEVER LEAVE US

I have been told that there are over 7,000 promises in the Bible. One of my favorites is found in Hebrews 13:5: "I will never leave you nor forsake you." Sounds good, doesn't it? But it's even better when you understand the full meaning. In the Greek language, in which the New Testament was written, there is what is called a triple negative. It is used when the author wants to be extremely emphatic. This is the only verse in the New Testament in which this triple negative is used, and literally translated it reads: "I will not, I will not, I will not, in any decree leave you helpless, nor forsake you, nor relax my hold on you, assuredly not." Now that's what I call a promise! And there are at least 6,999 more!

TO MAKE US CHRISTLIKE

Note Paul's familiar statement, "And we know that in all things God works for the good of those who love him, who have been called according to his purpose" (Rom. 8:28 NIV). Too frequently we stop there, ignoring the next verse. What is His purpose? "For those God foreknew he also predestined *to be conformed to the likeness of his Son*, that he might be the firstborn among many brothers" (Rom. 8:29 NIV, italics added).

True, all works together for good, but what is good? *Good* here is defined as "Christlikeness," as "possessing the fruit of the Holy Spirit in one's life." This fruit is described in Galatians 5:22–23 as love, joy, peace, patience, kindness, goodness, faithfulness, gentleness, and self-control, which is a good description of the inward qualities of the Proverb 31 woman. Wouldn't you like to possess these qualities? According to Romans 8:28–29, God is working in all the trials and joys of your marriage for this ultimate purpose, to develop in your life these beautiful qualities.

Consider Romans 5:2–5:

> And we rejoice in the hope of the glory of God. Not only so, but we also rejoice in our sufferings, because we know that suffering produces perseverance; perseverance, character; and character, hope. And hope does not disappoint us, because God has poured out his love into our hearts by the Holy Spirit, whom he has given us (NIV).

Have you considered your present situation in the light of God's eternal purpose?

Often the very things a woman resists and resents

are God's special tools to fashion her into the image of His Son. Even though she may not see the outcome now of an unruly child, an insensitive husband, a financial difficulty, or a sexual problem, she does see that God has not abandoned her, and she can be sure He has a definite, loving purpose in allowing this situation into her life. This perspective is fundamental to experiencing the power of the Holy Spirit.

NO TEMPTATION TOO GREAT

"No temptation has overtaken you except such as is common to man; but God is faithful, who will not allow you to be tempted beyond what you are able, but with the temptation will also make the way of escape, that you may be able to bear it" (1 Cor. 10:13). A woman may have problems in her personal life or her marriage that she feels are too heavy, too insurmountable. God promises that there is no temptation too great and that He will provide a way for her to endure it.

GOD'S CONSTANT CONCERN

"Casting all your care upon Him, for He cares for you" (1 Pet. 5:7). God wants each of us to cast all our problems and worries on His strong shoulders because He loves us and is concerned for us. How is this done? By choice of will.

A woman decides that the problem should be given to the Lord, and she simply *wills it* into His hands. Since human beings are so prone to unbelief, within two minutes of giving the problem to Him, she may find the old fears, doubts, and worries returning. It is as if she has given the problem to Him and then said, "Lord, let me take it back for a little while. I'm not confident You can really handle it. I think it will help the situation if I worry and fret about it for another day or so." But she needs to give it to Him and leave it in His hands. When the doubts return every two minutes, she needs to rededicate the problem to Him with another choice of will, and another, and another, and another until she finally feels that she has trusted it into His hands.

God will always be faithful to fulfill His promises. He has promised to be faithful to us, never to leave us, to give us the power and strength to live the Christian life. So how can we experience what God promises to do?

MAN'S 100 PERCENT

It can be summed up in one little verse: "Moreover it is required . . . that one be found faithful" (1 Cor. 4:2). The world says, "It is required that one be found successful, rich, famous, and attractive," but God requires only one thing: that each of us be faithful!

Does this remind you of the parable of the talents in Matthew 25? Jesus told the story of a man who was about to go on a long trip. The man called his servants and gave five silver coins (known as talents) to one of them, two talents to another, and one talent to a third.

Upon his return he again called the three servants to him, this time to evaluate what they had done with what had been given them. Discovering that the first servant had invested his five talents and now had ten, he praised him: "Well done, good and faithful servant; you were faithful over a few things, I will make you ruler over many things. Enter into the joy of your lord" (v. 21). The servant who had been given two talents also doubled his money, and he received similar praise. But the third servant had buried his one talent and had not multiplied it. He received not praise but great wrath from his master.

The issue here is not how many talents we have but how we use them. This is our part—to trust and obey. When we do, we begin to experience God working in us.

TRUST

Trust in what? We are to place our trust in a person—Jesus Christ. We are to trust Him for what He has already done and for what He promises to do. If we want to experience the release of the Spirit in our lives, we must begin to relate every circumstance and situation in our marriages to these promises. We must base our view of life on these promises, and a good way to begin to do that would be to memorize them.

For example, a hurtful situation in a marriage is no longer viewed as an irritating pain; instead it becomes attached to God's promises to make us Christlike by working through that hurt. The proper response is "in everything give thanks; for this is the will of God in Christ Jesus for you" (1 Thess. 5:18).

By faith, we must claim what God has promised as if it were ours already. How is this done? By coming to the Lord in prayer and verbally claiming the promise, by thanking Him for the promise and expressing our trust in Him that He is going to fulfill the promise in *His good and perfect time*. He knows what is best for us and will therefore see to it that the promise is fulfilled in the most perfect way. We do the possible by faith, trusting God to do the impossible.

One morning when the children were young, I was driving the first-grade car-pool to school. It was raining unexpectedly and fiercely. The streets were slick, I was tired, and the three children were quarreling in the back seat. (There seems to be something about car-pooling that brings out the fighting instincts in all small children!)

As I was driving down the winding road I was meditating on God's part and my part. Silently in prayer I told God that I hated to drive in the rain but that I wanted to do all I could—I wanted to be faithful to do my part. I knew only He could keep me and my three precious passengers safe.

I spoke to the children and the bickering stopped. I held the steering wheel tightly, turned on the lights, drove slowly, and stayed as alert as possible. Thirty seconds after I uttered my prayer I had a blowout. Ahead on the shoulder of the road was a space just big enough for my car—the only place within a mile where it was possible to pull off the road. And would you believe that directly across the street was the only gas station within miles? The attendant met me and the children at the door with, "Boy, lady, you sure are lucky! You could have had a bad accident!"

Lucky? No. Blessed? Definitely! Blessed by a loving Father who wants us to be faithful to do our part, and who over and over is faithful to do His part.

OBEY

The second aspect of faithfulness is consistent obedi-ence. We must not be like Mary, who is only "trusting" Jesus and never really obeying Him, nor are we to be like Susan, who is so totally focused on obedience that she becomes guilt ridden. We must trust *and* obey. That is our 100 percent.

Let's look at the story of Lazarus (see John 11). The brother of Mary and Martha and the beloved friend of Jesus had died and been buried for four days when Jesus arrived at his home in Bethany. Mary and Martha told Jesus through their tears that if He had been there, Lazarus would not have died. After asking them to show Him where they had laid Lazarus, Jesus directed them to roll back the large stone that secured the grave open-ing, and in a loud voice He commanded the dead man to come out. When Lazarus appeared in the doorway, still wrapped in the graveclothes, Jesus ordered the people to unwrap him.

Do you see the principle in this story? Jesus asked the people to do all the things they could do: show Him the grave, roll away the stone, unwrap the grave-clothes. And Jesus did what they could not do: raise Lazarus from the dead!

I have met a few Christians who literally await God's motivation. Occasionally a wife has told me that God has just not given her a feeling of love for her husband. God *does* give motivation, God *does* give feelings, but usually they come as a result of our obedience to Him. We must first make a decision of the will ("I will be the kind of wife God would have me be") and then *act,* step out in obedience to God. God promises He is at work within us doing His part. And that's exciting!

A LIFELONG PROCESS

Learning to obey and to trust is a process that takes repetition and discipline. God wants to make you a *creative counterpart* to your husband. He wants the finished product to be His work. He wants you to trust Him. Your trust comes from a certain knowledge of your own inability to live it; your obedience comes from the confidence that if you obey and trust, He will fulfill His promise, and His Spirit will mold you into His image.

It is a process that takes a lifetime. If God wants to grow a cabbage, He can do it in a few weeks, but if He wants to grow an oak tree, He has decreed that it will take Him a lifetime. God is trying to produce oak-tree Christians—Christians who have deep roots, who have learned obedience, who have strong trunks that are not easily swayed by winds or trials. Settle on His ultimate objective and purpose in your heart to be faithful to trust and obey now! That's your part. His part is to do what He has promised in His own way and in His own time through the power of the Holy Spirit.

By now you may be protesting, "I thought this was a book on how to be a *creative counterpart.* You haven't been talking about my marriage. You have been discussing my relationship with God! Maybe I picked up the wrong book!" You thought you were going to learn how to be creative, loving, organized, and all the other attributes that will make your marriage a love affair. You are! But in the process you will be bombarded with your responsibilities as a wife, mother, woman, and Christian, and that can be overwhelming. So first you need to focus on your relationship with God and on His faithfulness. Look at God, at how He is at work in your life, molding you, changing you, encouraging you, helping you. God will never give up on you, even on those days when you wail, "I'll never be a *creative counterpart!*" God wants you to be a *creative counterpart.* He is there, and He will never leave you nor forsake you.

Now, armed with His promises, let's begin!

⟡ 4 ⟡

The Priority Planner

A friend of mine took the words of Psalm 90:12—
"So teach us to number our days, / That we may gain
a heart of wisdom"—seriously and totaled up the number of days she would have left on earth if she lived
to be seventy. She was thirty at the time, and she discovered that the remaining forty years would give her
14,600 days. She was greatly challenged and motivated
by this discovery: forty years seemed like a long time
until she saw the time broken down into days and realized how swiftly life passes. She resolved then to live
each day to the fullest. But her zeal lasted for about a
week, and then she forgot about it. When she remembered and again numbered her days, several years had
passed and she discovered that she had only 12,000
days remaining! *Where did they go?* she asked herself.
What did I do with those 2,600 days?

What *do* we do with our days? Our male counterparts
always seem to know what they're doing with theirs.
A man is generally more goal oriented than a woman;
a man usually has his life laid out before him and knows
where he is heading: in five years he will be a division
manager in his company, in ten years he will start his
own business, and in fifteen he will make a million
dollars!

How many women have plans like that? How many women just let one day flow into the next, the days into weeks, and the weeks into months until another year has passed? Is New Year's Day a time of satisfied reflection for you, or are you like my neighbor, who remarked to me one January that she couldn't think of anything she had accomplished in the past year?

At the end of his life the apostle Paul was able to say, "I have fought the good fight, I have finished the race. . . . Finally, there is laid up for me the crown of righteousness" (2 Tim. 4:7–8). Too often a woman approaches the end of life and inwardly laments, *I've fought a mediocre fight as a wife and mother. I didn't run well in my race.* What a tragedy! But you can do something about your life *now.*

What is your goal in life? Do you even have one? Perhaps you don't think in terms of a lifetime because your concern is getting the laundry done this week or preparing tonight's dinner. Take a minute right now, and write in one paragraph or less your life goal. I've thought a lot about this and have decided that, simply stated, my goal is to be a godly woman, to be all that God wants me to be as a woman, wife, and mother.

Sounds good on paper, doesn't it? But how am I going to fill this big order? Think for a minute with me. What areas of responsibility make up a woman's world? Write down your answers. I came up with the areas of children, husband, God, self, home, and a job or other outside activities. Now that we have identified these areas, how are we going to organize them into priorities so that we can live each day to the fullest and grow more like the virtuous wife of Proverb 31? The rest of this chapter shares the organizational plan I have developed to help us reach this goal.

THE PRIORITY PLANNER 49

PRIORITY #1—GOD

But seek first the kingdom of God and His righteousness, and all these things shall be added to you (Matt. 6:33).

The relationship with God must come first. Why? Because we need God's perspective in every other area of our lives. We see this in His commands to us: "But seek first his kingdom and his righteousness, and all these things will be given to you as well" (Matt. 6:33 NIV) and " 'You shall love the LORD your God with all your heart, with all your soul, and with all your mind.' This is the first and great commandment" (Matt. 22:37–38). God knows we need to spend time with Him to get to know Him and to learn His game plan for our lives.

One of the biggest and most common mistakes a woman makes is to substitute *activity* for God for a *relationship* with Him. On the outside, she is busy running the holy hurdles, but on the inside, her relationship with Christ is at a standstill.

I have always been able to identify with Martha in the New Testament. When Jesus visited Martha and Mary and Lazarus, Mary sat at His feet to learn from Him (see Luke 10:39). (Mary was mentioned five times in the New Testament, and each time she was at the feet of Jesus.) But Martha was scurrying around, preparing food, attending to the guests, tidying the house. Martha was the organizer. Martha's contributions *were* important, yet when she complained to Jesus that Mary was not helping her, He replied that Mary had "chosen that good part, which will not be taken away from her" (Luke 10:42).

Christ was not saying that organizing, cooking, and serving are not important. They are, and we can receive much joy from doing these things. Yet all the activity in the world will never give us the peace and joy of a vital relationship with Jesus Christ. We need to spend more time sitting at the feet of Jesus.

To know Jesus in a personal way, we need to zero in on four major areas: prayer, Bible study, devotional time, and fellowship.

TALKING WITH GOD

If I talked with Jody only between eleven and twelve on Sunday morning, how well would I know him? Prayer, talking with God, is vital in building an exciting relationship with Jesus Christ. First Thessalonians 5:17 says we are to pray without ceasing, but no one can pray all the time! What this verse describes is an attitude of prayer. I think of it in this way: whenever my mind is disengaged (such as when I clean a bathtub), my thoughts can go to prayer instead of to resentment, anxiety, or frustration. I can thank God for my children as I load the dishwasher, and I can ask His help as I drive the car-pool to school.

Mark 1:35 describes Jesus getting up early to meet with His Father. This seems to indicate that a Christian needs specific times of prayer with God in addition to the short prayers lifted up throughout the day. Prayer is hard work, so an individual may try to avoid it. There are so many things to pray about that she is afraid if she ever got down on her knees, she'd never get up! Sometimes she has good intentions to pray, but life gets hectic and days pass without her taking time to pray. It becomes one of those I'll-do-it-tomorrow things.

My friend Peggy taught me that two praying together can break through the I'll-pray-later barrier. Our family had been transplanted for three months to Illinois where Jody was a visiting professor in a graduate school. Our three children were all in school, and when I was not team teaching with Jody, I was free—a three-month interlude in my life when I had lots of time to pray, right? Wrong! Until Peggy announced that she would descend on my doorstep two mornings a week at 8:30 to pray with me. We had an "appointment to pray." What joy to see God answer specific prayer! Especially to see Him show Jody and me that we would soon be moving to Vienna, Austria.

Throughout the years, I have continued to make appointments to pray. I met with another friend, Judy, over a year-and-a-half period to specifically pray for wisdom and guidance with our teenagers.

Having appointments with friends has helped me to have more appointments to pray—just God and me. We are all weak human beings; therefore we all need help.

What will help you? My friend Claudia makes lists and prays over them. Shirley writes prayers in individual notebooks for her husband and her children. Debby writes a journal of prayers to God. One imaginative Christian friend uses the days of the week as guidelines for her prayer life. Using this pattern, she feels everyone gets prayed for!

Monday	—	missionaries
Tuesday	—	tasks
Wednesday	—	wants and needs
Thursday	—	thanksgiving
Friday	—	friends

Saturday   —   saints
Sunday   —   sinners

"All right," you say. "But how do I do it? I don't think I can come up with enough churchy phrases to keep going!" Relax. God doesn't want a recital of the prayer book; He wants you to be yourself. He wants you to use the words you normally use in talking with your friends or with your husband. (Since He's your Father, you can even call Him "You" instead of "Thou"!) He also wants you to be specific. Instead of saying, "Thank You for all my many blessings," try praying, "Thank You for providing the extra money we needed to pay our medical bills this month."

God longs for each of us to bring to Him the things that really make us happy or that really cause us concern. Nothing is too small for His attention; nothing is out of His realm; no matter is inappropriate for His ears. One wife came to me seeking counsel about her sexual relationship with her husband. After some discussion I asked her if she had ever prayed about it. She recoiled in shock and gasped, "Oh, no! I don't talk to God about things like *that!*" How sadly ironic that we creatures of the Creator feel He wouldn't understand certain parts of our lives. Our heavenly Father knows us inside out and longs to talk with us about every detail of our existence.

LIKE NEWBORN BABIES

We need to listen to God speak through the Scriptures as well as to converse with Him in prayer. Like newborn babies we are to "desire the pure milk of the word" so that we may grow by taking it in (1 Pet. 2:2). Anyone who has experienced motherhood knows that a baby doesn't quietly and meekly request his milk, "If it wouldn't be too much trouble for you, please." He screams, he wails, he rages until the milk is within reach, and then he lunges for it in desperation and drinks ravenously. He acts as though he'll starve to death if there is a delay of one second longer! This should be our attitude toward the Word. Nothing else will truly satisfy the hunger of our inward selves. Our problem is that we don't always realize how hungry we are.

God also says His Book will be a lamp for our feet and a light for our path. Everything we need to know about God, ourselves, and life has been written in God's love letter to us. The rich truths of God's Word have been compared to gold in a mine, with the big problem being how to dig them out! Today we are blessed with an abundance of exciting study guides, Bible hand-books, and commentaries to help us with our investiga-tion, but these are only tools to aid us and should not be substituted for our own deep inspection of the Word.

What are the results of such study? As a woman, I can see that my life is changed as I see more of who God is. As I more fully understand His character, I can trust Him on a deeper level with my life, my mar-riage, and my children. As a mother, I can give my children answers concerning life and death and heaven and eternity, as well as things in the here and now. My children will realize the importance of God's Word only as I answer their questions from it.

I remember when Joy was seven and a neighbor, the mother of two young boys, became ill and lay near death for several weeks. Our family prayed for her and tried to help the father and sons, but my daughter didn't want to pray for her and refused to talk about her illness. I wondered what I had done wrong to produce such a heartless child. Later that week, I arrived home after teaching a seminar to find gifts my children had made for me. Among my daughter's drawings was a letter. It read, "Dear Mommy, I love you. I love you very much. I hope you never die. Love, Joy."

Her seeming lack of sensitivity was actually fear that her mommy would also get sick and die. I took her in my arms and shared with her what God's Word said about life and death. We had talked about those things before, but they took on real meaning in that situation.

As our children grow, they are bombarded from every side by the world's perspective. Our daughters are in a high school where the Christian population is very low. In Vienna the legal drinking age is fifteen; the swimming pools are topless, obviously not the atmosphere I would choose for my teens; and all they have been taught is questioned by their peers. Often I thank God that I know His Word and can give my teenagers answers about life from Him! And how He has challenged me with the realization that I can give my children no more than I have myself!

INTO THE CLOSET

The best time to build a relationship with Christ through prayer and Bible study is during a devotional time. I know how many of us really struggle with this! We manage to carve out the time for maybe a week, and then we give up. I think one reason for our failure is that we set our goals too high: "I'll be up every morning at six!'' I've tried this, and by the third day I'm so exhausted that I can't even find the Bible, let alone study it!

God wants us to be realistic. When I had young children, it was realistic for me to be up early three mornings a week to spend time with Him. The other days I had a quiet time while my children were resting. With four teenagers, I can pick my time during the day when they are gone. Evaluate your life and set a goal that is realistic for you. Don't feel guilty if you read about some dear saint who gets up at five every morning to pray for her nine children! A devotional time is not a law but a relationship. Your relationship with the Savior will be different from everyone else's.

Your quiet time is a time for you to draw apart with God. It is a special time for you to talk over with Him the events of the day, your growth in Him, your concerns, your blessings. A quiet time is not a time to prepare your Sunday school lesson. Neither is it a time to browse through a church magazine or even to write to your missionary.

It is a time to set aside to deepen your knowledge of the Lord, to enrich your personal relationship with Him, to fellowship with Him, to love Him, to worship Him on a very personal basis. This quiet time each day is for *your own personal growth* in the Lord. No matter how old you are in the Lord or how closely you walk with Him, I feel this time of intimate fellowship will always be necessary.

You may have a set time for it, or it may happen several times during the day. You may take five minutes or five hours, as the Spirit and circumstances lead, but vital personal contact with the Lord is necessary so

that you may have a constant inpouring of the life of
Christ, and so that He may channel it through you to
others. Do not ever feel you must stick to rules and
regulations in order to achieve this. Try being creative!
My friend Phyllis spends one morning a week in prayer
and Bible study. She goes away from her home so she
won't be distracted by a ringing phone, unwashed
clothes, or a creative project. Another friend goes to a
coffee shop daily to have a time alone with the Lord.
If you desire to know Him better, the Holy Spirit will
certainly lead you in your efforts.[1]

FELLOWSHIP

What do you do when at age thirty-two you find
yourself divorced and your children in your husband's
custody? You could commit suicide, blame God, pity
yourself, or eat yourself into obesity. Betty chose another path. Committing herself to Christ and trusting
Him to work good out of tragedy, she sought help from
other Christians.

"My Christian friends saw my need and fulfilled it
to the point of self-sacrifice," she told me. "They believed in me as a person, accepted me as I was, but
had a vision for what I could become. I had families
to live with, brothers and sisters who provided my inner
and outer needs."

Wilma's pain was physical. As a college student, she
discovered she had a serious illness, and now she lives
with daily pain and discomfort. No one can help her
physical pain, but the body of Christ has ministered
to Wilma by reminding her of God's eternal perspective—a "ministry of reminding" her to apply God's
truths to her daily walk. "Therefore, I will not be negli-

gent to remind you always of these things, though you know them, and are established in the present truth" (2 Pet. 1:12).

Fellowship has a deeper meaning than mere friendship; the Greek word for it is *koinonia*, which means "sharing in common." We desperately need to share our Christian experience with others who believe and likewise allow them to share with us. "Under his [Christ's] direction the whole body is fitted together perfectly, and each part in its own special way helps the other parts, so that the whole body is healthy and growing and full of love" (Eph. 4:16 TLB).

In the body of Christ there is no age. Some of my richest fellowship has been with women twice my age, and encouragement and spiritual insight have often been given to me by my children.

I always longed for a sister, and God has given me special sisters in Christ to encourage, exhort, and build me up. "And let us consider one another in order to stir up love and good works" (Heb. 10:24).

PRIORITY #2—HUSBAND

An excellent wife is the crown of her husband (Prov. 12:4).

Solomon said, "A worthy wife is her husband's joy and crown; the other kind corrodes his strength and tears down everything he does" (Prov. 12:4 TLB). Did you catch that? A "worthy wife" versus "the other kind." Solomon said that there are only two kinds of wives, and you're either one or the other. No gray area here. You're either a joy or a destroyer.

Solomon also said, "A wise woman builds her house, while a foolish woman tears hers down by her own efforts" (Prov. 14:1 TLB). Perhaps the foolish woman's efforts are really a lack of effort; she gets in a rut and just stops making an effort. What have you done creatively this week to make your marriage a love affair? Not last Valentine's Day but this *week*. Let's look at some of the positive things a wise woman, a *creative counterpart*, does to build her relationship with the most important man in her life.

I LOVE YOU—PERIOD!

The most-used word in the English language today must be *love*, but how is that word really used? A woman may say, "I love you *if* you perform the way I want you to." Or "I love you, *and* I expect this in return." Or "I love you, *but* don't you get too close." Or "I love you *because* of the status and security you offer." *If*, *and*, *but*, or *because*—is this the way God loves us? The most exciting thing I've ever learned is that God loves me—period! He loves me unconditionally. God sent His Son to die for you and me while we were yet sinners—not after we had shaped our lives up! And guess what? God asks us to love our husbands as He loves us. Unconditionally, with no strings attached.

I remember when, as a new Christian in college, I first came face to face with God's love for me. I didn't know much of what was in the Bible, but I did know 1 Corinthians 13, and I read it over and over, basking in what it told me:

Love is patient, love is kind. It does not envy, it does not boast, it is not proud. It is not rude, it is

not self-seeking, it is not easily angered, it keeps
no record of wrongs. Love does not delight in evil
but rejoices with the truth. It always protects, always
trusts, always hopes, always perseveres. Love never
fails (vv. 4–8 NIV).

I thought this passage was one of the most beautiful I
had ever read until one day a friend suggested I go
home and read it, putting my name where the word
love appeared, to see if this was the kind of love I
had for my new husband. So I started out, "Linda is
patient, Linda is kind." (Gulp.) "She does not envy,
she does not boast, she is not proud." (Oh, no.) "Linda
is not rude, she is not self-seeking, she is not easily
angered." And so I went, until I was completely sobered
by my responsibility to love as God loves me. Try this
yourself sometime with a heart receptive to God's speaking to you. This kind of love is not an option. It's a
requirement.

WHO'S FIRST IN YOUR HEART?

When Joy was three, she came to me one day with
a baited question, "Mommy, who do you love most,
Jesus or me?" I knew she wouldn't understand if I answered, "Jesus," so after some quick thinking I replied,
"Honey, I love Jesus the most of the people in heaven,
and I love Daddy, you, Robin, and Tommy the most
of the people here on earth." She liked my answer,
and she said, "Me, too! That's the way I love them,
too!"

Do you show your husband that of all of the people
here on earth you love him the most? Is he sure he's
first in your heart? Before you have children and after

the children leave home, it is easier to keep your husband first in your heart since there are not other family members vying for your attention or time. The hardest times in our marriage have been when we had three little ones and later when we had four teenagers. With little ones, I was physically exhausted, and with teenagers, I felt emotionally exhausted, which led to physical tiredness. During both stages in my life, I have had to work at keeping my husband first.

I first learned this important lesson when we moved to Philadelphia. Tommy was five weeks old, Robin was eighteen months, and Joy had just turned three. Not only was I a walking zombie, but my priorities kept getting tangled. In my heart and mind Jody was first, but my actions never seemed to illustrate that. Every time he wanted to sit and talk with me, some little person needed a diaper changed, needed to be fed, or had some major catastrophe! The children's needs were so immediate, so pressing. I wanted to be a good mother, but I also wanted to be a good wife. So I began to pray that God would show me at this difficult time in my life how to let Jody know he was first in my heart.

HOW ABOUT A DATE, HONEY?

The first thing God showed me was that Jody and I needed to have dates. You remember what dating is—that's what you did *before* you were married! You went out *alone* together for an entire evening. At that time Jody and I were going to a couples Bible study he taught on Tuesday evenings. So instead of getting the baby sitter at seven-thirty, we started having her come at four-thirty or five-thirty, and we would spend two or three hours just talking.

When we had the money (which wasn't often), we would go out to dinner. Other times we took a picnic supper, and sometimes we sat in a restaurant and had a cup of coffee. Some of our most memorable times have been spent over a cup of coffee, not by spending money but by communicating with each other. I feel a couple should try to have a date every two weeks, or every week if possible. A wonderful tool to encourage dating and also to spur in-depth conversation is the book *Ten Dates for Mates* by Dave and Claudia Arp (Thomas Nelson, 1983). I highly recommend you try it. Are you moaning, "How will we ever find the time?" One thing I've learned in my twenty-two years of married life is that you can do anything that is important to you!

ALONE AT LAST

As I prayed and thought of ways to show Jody he was first in my life, the second thing I realized was that we needed extended time together, away from the children, a kind of second honeymoon. Being short on both money and baby sitters, I decided to turn this one over to the Lord. I couldn't arrange it, but I knew He could. A few days later a friend, a medical doctor and the mother of five children, mentioned she had a key to a lovely apartment belonging to a fellow doctor who traveled extensively. She asked if I knew anyone in need of a place to stay. I held out my hand! By arranging to trade off with another set of parents, we got baby-sitting for our children, and then we were off for a wonderful twenty-four hours together.

Three words come to mind as I reflect on our weekend retreats: *pray, plan,* and *persevere.* Once we had a three-day getaway all planned. We even got the baby sitter to spend the night at our house so that I could catch the 6:30 A.M. bus and join Jody in the city where he was speaking. At 2:00 A.M. our youngest child became violently ill, and the trip had to be canceled. Shortly after that we tried again, and the baby sitter got sick! ("Lord," I said, "I prayed for us and for the children but forgot the baby sitter. Next time she'll be first on my list!") It *is* a hassle to get off alone on a date or a weekend retreat, but don't give up. Just remember to pray, plan, and persevere!

LITTLE THINGS MEAN A LOT

When was the last time you sent a note to your husband at his job, thanking him for taking you out to dinner? Or put a note in his briefcase or lunch box telling him you love him? It only costs a few cents to send a letter, and it only takes a few minutes to write one. You probably write thank-you notes to everybody—to the neighbors who invited your family over for hot dogs, to Aunt Grace who sent the lovely ceramic poodle candy dish, and to Mrs. Duzitall who so generously gave of her time to speak at your meeting. But what about the fellow who takes you out to dinner when he'd rather collapse on the sofa, who sends you roses even though they make his nose itch, and who spends Saturday afternoons watching your offspring play soccer when the football game on television beckons him?

Don't assume that your husband just *knows* you appreciate him. Try letting him know by writing or by saying it explicitly. He may not show any emotion or he may even act embarrassed, but inside he'll be thinking you're a pretty smart woman to have figured out what a terrific guy he is. There are hundreds of little things you can say and do to let him know you love him. Use your imagination; creativity doesn't cost money!

One clever, imaginative wife takes the prize for the most creative Valentine's Day gift. She and her husband had grave financial problems and no money available for extras like fancy gifts. On Valentine's Day, she brought her husband a tray with his favorite breakfast, a long-stemmed rose in a vase, and a card that read, "Happy Valentine's Day, Darling! In lieu of a gift, contributions have been made in your name to: (1) the electric company, (2) the telephone company, (3) MasterCard."

CREATIVE CHRISTMAS

Before we had our children, Christmas and Jody's birthday were creative times for me. One year I saved $150 to buy him an overhead projector for Christmas. To get the money I gave (sold) blood, had our high-school rings melted and then sold the gold, and schemed and connived anyway I could. I was so excited about the projector that I almost gave it to him before Christmas! The gift meant a lot to Jody, not because it was expensive but because he knew the time, effort, and love that had gone into it.

But after you have children it's such fun to buy dolls and trains, and somehow your husband doesn't seem as important anymore. Realizing this had happened to me, I began to ask God to show me something creative to give Jody for Christmas that would convey my love and appreciation for him. I knew I couldn't sell blood (after having three children in three years, I didn't have much left!), and we didn't have any more rings to melt, so I figured $50 was the most I could spend.

I knew that getting him something really nice for $50 would be a challenge because Jody doesn't really have an interest in new clothes or anything like that. He likes books—so many books that we could almost open a public library in our house! That year I discovered by some carefully veiled questioning that his heart's secret desire was a set of scholarly commentaries selling for the low, low price of only $130. Fighting the urge to give up and just buy him a tie, I called the bookstore to find out if the books were still in print and if I could buy them one at a time. The nice man in the store replied that they were sold only as a set, but that I was in luck. They were on sale for the rock-bottom price of only $115!

I thanked him and had the receiver halfway back to the hook when he inquired, "Lady, do you *really* want those books?"

"I really do," I replied.

"Well, wait a minute," he said. "I think another fellow who works here has a set he might want to sell."

The other fellow came to the phone and asked if I were sure I wanted the books. He said they were very deep, and he had given up trying to read them. I assured him my husband would *love* them!

"Well, would $50 be too much?" he asked hesitantly. "They're still in the original boxes, but I *have* made one mark in them."

I managed to stay calm while making arrangements to pick them up. Then after I hung up, I literally shouted to God with a voice of praise, thanking Him that He was concerned that my husband know he was first in my life!

GET THAT GRAY MATTER PERKING

The results of a recent survey revealed that husbands usually list a lack of variety as the main problem in marriage. They may love their wives, but they're still just plain bored. Remember the question I asked earlier: What have you done creatively this week to make your marriage a love affair?

I thought my busy life made it hard to be creative until I was struck by the example of a friend. Nancy's husband was a resident at a local hospital, working thirty-six hours and then having twelve hours off. For this he received four hundred dollars a month. Since this wasn't enough for them to live on, he would work at other hospitals on his weekends off in order to make ends meet. The result was that they saw each other about as often as you and I see the president!

But unlike many of her friends in medical circles, Nancy refused to let this demanding schedule ruin their marriage. On Friday evenings when Jim couldn't come home, she would dress up their daughter and herself and would drive forty-five minutes across town in rush-hour traffic to have dinner with him in the hospital cafeteria. How many of the other wives do you think did this? Right! Jim would proudly show off his wife and little girl to all his colleagues who were munching their meat loaf and macaroni in solitude. Warmed by her demonstration of love, he would then go back to work while Nancy drove the long miles home.

On Thanksgiving, when all the other men in America

were home with their families and turkey dinners and football games on TV, Jim had to work. Undaunted, Nancy packed up the turkey and trimmings, the linen and silver, and took the whole works to the hospital, where she and Jim dined in "elegance."

As I shared this story in a seminar, a woman in the audience blurted out, "How dumb!" Yes, I suppose you could look at it that way. I mean, it was a lot of trouble carting a hot turkey across town, and they must have looked a little strange sitting there eating in the hospital, but what do you think it communicated to Nancy's husband? As she continued to do things like this, he was assured that he was more important to her than anything else, and that when he couldn't come to her, she would come to him.

And another interesting thing happened in their marriage. Nancy was a new Christian, very excited about her faith. Jim was skeptical and watched her carefully. She could have sermonized, preached, and nagged, but instead she just loved him. Before long, he, too, was excited about the Christian life!

Wherever you are in life, it will be difficult to keep your love affair with your husband alive. I sometimes feel after juggling the activities and needs of four very active teens that there is nothing left to give. How easy to say, "Oh, Jody understands how tired I am. In a few short years we'll be alone together and then . . ." But what will we have left of our relationship, our love affair, if it is neglected now? Jody must be Priority #2—now!

PRIORITY #3—CHILDREN

Children are a gift from God (Ps. 127:3 TLB).

In Isaiah 28:9–10 we read,

> Whom will he teach knowledge?
> And whom will he make to understand the message?
> Those just weaned from milk?
> Those just drawn from the breasts?
> For precept must be upon precept,
>   precept upon precept,
> Line upon line, line upon line,
> Here a little, there a little.

I wish I could have sat my children down and in one lesson taught them all there is to know about character, godliness, manners, life, and death. Wouldn't that be nice? Unfortunately, it doesn't happen quite that way. I must give them, as Isaiah says, here a little, there a little, precept upon precept, line upon line. So many times I feel nothing is going past their ears into their minds. Then hark—I'll see some small grain of truth that has penetrated, encouraging me to continue giving line upon line!

LIKE MOTHER, LIKE DAUGHTER

The book of Ezekiel states that what the mother is, the daughter will turn out to be (see 16:44). I groaned when I read that! The most challenging job I have ever undertaken is being a mother! I thought I was a patient, relatively organized person until I had three small children. I then thought I'd learned a lot about patience until I had four teens. I'm convinced some of God's greatest tools to form us into His image are our own children.

What we are speaks so much louder than what we

say. In Deuteronomy we find we must practice what we preach: "And these words, which I command you today shall be in your heart; you shall teach them diligently to your children, and shall talk of them when you sit in your house, when you walk by the way, when you lie down, and when you rise up" (6:6–7).

Unless you have a vital relationship with God, it is impossible to impart His truth to your children as you sit in the house, walk by the way, lie down, and rise up. These verses depict a parent whose love and commitment to God are so much a part of her life that she shares and relates this wisdom and law of God to every life situation. Your children are watching. What are they seeing in your life?

AM I REALLY THERE?

When my children were young, I had a conversation with a gracious Christian woman whose children were nearly grown. She commented, "Linda, you teach seminars, speak, and so forth. My, you must be out of your home a great deal of the time."

I piously replied, "No, I only allow myself two mornings a week out of my home. I'm home with my children the majority of the time."

The dear woman sighed and said, "I could have said that, too, when I was your age. But, you know, if I had it to do over again, I'd do it so differently. I was in my home all right, but I wasn't *really* there! I was on the phone planning a luncheon, organizing the Sunday school program or a tennis tournament. And when my children came into the room, I'd shove cookies in their hands and tell them Mommy was busy."

Oh, Lord, I thought, *I've given a few cookies!*

God used this discussion to challenge me to evaluate my time with my children. Was I really there—available for their needs? Or was I preoccupied with other things in order to avoid the pressure and responsibility of small children? It was a sobering reflection. Even the tastiest cookie is no substitute for time and attention.

I would like to especially recommend two books to you. *Sanity in the Summertime* (Thomas Nelson, 1981), which my friend Claudia Arp and I wrote, helps mothers plan a step-by-step procedure for enduring and strengthening relationships with children during the summer months. Claudia's book *Almost Thirteen* (Thomas Nelson, 1986) is a must for any mother of a child who is nearing those teenage years.

OH SUSANNA

A woman in history who has greatly challenged me as a mother was named Susanna. She had nineteen children (a feat I feel deserves the Medal of Honor!) at a time when women nursed their babies for years. The way I figure it, this dear woman must have been either pregnant or nursing a baby her entire adult life!

She also lived at a time when there were no Kentucky Fried Chicken, no Hamburger Helper, and no Duncan Hines. Everything was made from scratch. No school was available for her children (the nine who survived into their school years), so she taught them herself. (Wouldn't that be fun?) Susanna's husband traveled, and we all know how that helps life on the home front!

In a letter to her husband, Susanna related that she felt it an awesome responsibility before God to raise the children for Him. She said she had decided to spend time one evening a week with each child individually, and named the child and the night. Some nights she had to double up, since she had more than seven children. (I thought, *Oh, I'm so tired at night, how did she do it? This woman's self-sacrifice is overwhelming!*) Susanna also related that on some days she was so concerned for her children to become the men and women God wanted that she would spend an hour a day in prayer for them.

Were this mother's time, prayer, and self-sacrifice worthwhile? Susanna's last name was Wesley. Two of her sons, John and Charles, grew up and transformed England by a social and spiritual revolution.

FIRST ON THE CRITICAL LIST

Psychologists say the most important thing a mother can do for her child is to love the child's father, and the most important thing a father can do for his child is to love the child's mother. A child can be loved by the mother and loved by the father, but if Mommy and Daddy don't love each other, a child can have deep feelings of insecurity. Priority #2 (our husbands) and Priority #3 (our children) must be in their proper places.

PRIORITY #4—HOME

She watches over the ways of her household,
And does not eat the bread of idleness (Prov. 31:27).

The virtuous wife in Proverb 31 seems to have been a very neat, tidy housekeeper. It seems to come naturally to some people, but I'm not one of them. I remember years ago visiting a friend, and as our children began to play I realized every toy her children owned was still in the box it had come in! At our house, the original boxes were gone, and many of the toys had missing parts. I keep working on my clutterbug tendencies, but it's still hard for me.

YOU SET THE PACE

Because of the woman she was, our friend in Proverb 31 had a home that exuded a good atmosphere, making it a place people wanted to frequent. Every home has an atmosphere. Maybe you don't know what the atmosphere of your home is, but there are some who do— the people who frequent it. How would you describe the atmosphere in your home? Pick an adjective: *warm, peaceful, loving, cheerful, united?* How about *anxious, bitter, contentious,* or *frustrated?*

It is the woman in each home who creates the atmosphere. She is like the hub of the wheel around which the home revolves. Have you ever noticed how quickly your husband and children pick up your moods? When you're grumpy, your husband seems to come home grumpy, too, and your children pick up that mood the second they come in from school. Then you wonder what is the matter with them!

Try it tonight. An experiment in terror. Be a real first-class Oscar the Grouch at dinner time, and see how long it takes the others to follow suit. Better yet, be the woman God wants you to be, and see how fast they respond positively!

WHAT! ME ORGANIZED?

Sometimes a woman is criticized for taking thirty minutes to do something that should take ten. Many times the criticism is deserved. Because a woman in the home has the freedom to budget her time as she likes, often she cops out and doesn't budget at all.

Several years ago I began to make out what I call my priority sheet, listing my priorities in a column along with my daily schedule, weekly schedule, and menu list. (See sample sheet on the next page.) Because this idea encouraged me, I have shared it with many others. It has worked for them, too. So I put together the *Priority Planner* (Thomas Nelson, 1977), a fifty-two-page booklet of double sheets with a perforated shopping list designed to help Christian women keep their priorities straight and be more efficient in the home.[2]

Sunday evening is a good planning time for me. I begin by listing one special project under each priority. Perhaps a candlelight dinner for Jody and a family slide show for the children. Next I transfer the special project under each priority to the appropriate place on the weekly schedule. Then, I fill in the major things to do for that week on the weekly schedule. Finally, I make out the daily schedule each evening. All this daily and weekly planning may seem burdensome, but planning enables me to accomplish more in less time.

Charles Schwab, one of the first presidents of the Bethlehem Steel Company, realized the value of planning, and he asked an efficiency expert, Ivy Lee, to come up with a method to pep up his employees to do the things they needed to do. Schwab said he would pay anything within reason.

Mr. Lee promised to give him something to step up his production by at least 50 percent. Handing Schwab a blank piece of paper, Ivy Lee instructed him to do the following: (1) write down the six most important tasks you have to do tomorrow, and number them in order of importance; (2) first thing tomorrow begin with item one and stick with it until you're finished; (3) after completing number one, cross it out with a bright red pen; and (4) proceed to number two and complete it before going on to three.

After trying this method for a few weeks, Schwab sent Ivy Lee a check for $25,000 with a letter saying the lesson was the most profitable he had ever learned.

After only five years, this plan was credited as a major factor in turning the unknown Bethlehem Steel Company into the biggest independent steel producer in the world. And it helped Charles Schwab make $100 million![3]

Now, I won't promise you $100 million, but I am convinced you will be a more organized, happier person if you use the $25,000 plan. I have made use of this plan by writing it in the boxes marked "Daily Schedule" in the *Priority Planner*.

I plan my menus as I work through my priority list and weekly schedule. Then I make out the shopping list for the week. I do all this with my *Priority Planner*, and I tear off the shopping list Monday morning as I head out the door on my way to the store.

Perhaps this method of planning would be helpful to you, too. If not, find one that will. The important thing is that you be faithful and do all things decently and orderly.

I'm convinced that much of a woman's frustration in the home stems from disorganization and inefficient use of time. She putters around, getting little accomplished, and then complains because she never has the time to do the things she enjoys. Wise use of the *Priority Planner* can change this!

Priorities/*Week of*

1 LORD • *"But seek first His kingdom and His righteousness; and all these things shall be added to you."*   *Matt. 6:33*
   Memorize 3 verses

2 HUSBAND • *"An excellent wife is the crown of her husband..."*   *Prov. 12:4*
   Candlelight dinner

3 CHILDREN • *"Behold, children are a gift of the Lord."*   *Psalm 127:3*
   Popcorn
   Slides of family

4 HOME • *"She looks well to the ways of her household, and does not eat the bread of idleness."*   *Prov. 31:27*
   Paint bedroom

5 YOURSELF • *"You shall love your neighbor as yourself."*   *Matt. 19:19*
   Jog
   Crochet shawl

6 OUTSIDE THE HOME • *"Go therefore and make disciples of all nations..."*   *Matt. 28:19*
   Bible study
   Meeting

Things To Do This Week

Bring flowers to Grandma

Take dog to vet

Weekly Schedule

Monday
Begin shawl
Kids slides

Tuesday
Meeting

Wednesday
Bible study

Thursday

Friday
Candlelight dinner

Saturday
Paint bedroom

Sunday
Church

Daily Schedule	Menu	Shopping List
Get yarn - shawl Grocery Make fruit cocktail Jog Write 2 letters Get slides ready	Tacos, frozen fruit cocktail	Taco sauce Ground beef Carrots Strawberries Chicken French bread Pot roast Cereal Detergent Cat food
	Baked fish, potatoes, salad, carrots	
	BBQ beef sandwiches french fries	
	Chicken in the Pot	
	Roast, potatoes, strawberry salad	
	Chicken-rice casserole	
	Spaghetti, French bread, green beans, salad	

A PAIN OR A CHALLENGE

Do you consider it a pain in the neck or a challenge to plan exciting meals in spite of the high prices caused by inflation? Recently I arrived home from the grocery store and began unpacking three mammoth grocery bags. Jody walked in, and I began the barrage. "Honey, would you believe what oatmeal costs!" "Honey, would you believe I paid $1.50 for this box of cereal?"

After several items, I stopped and said, "I sound like the contentious woman in Proverbs, don't I?" I realized I was griping about prices and complaining to Jody when there was nothing he could do about it. He gives me as much money as he can, and it is my responsibility to create delicious, colorful, and nutritious meals with the money I have—without griping. Solomon said, "It is better to dwell in a corner of a housetop, / Than in a house shared with a contentious woman" (Prov. 25:24).

I read of one woman who, after concocting a meatless, high-protein, good-for-you casserole of grated potatoes, carrots, onions, powdered milk, and eggs, was eager for her husband's opinion. After eating a few forkfuls, he commented, "Well, it's just fine, Honey, but I wouldn't want it every year!"

Now I must praise the invention of the Crock Pot, the greatest boon to a busy wife the world has ever known! Mine has been a true blessing! As I'm writing now, my Crock Pot is at home cooking a round steak that will be completely ready for dinner tonight. It's terrific knowing that dinner is taken care of. I can cook several chicken dishes, roasts, casseroles, or just about anything in it. Usually I cook two meals at once and freeze one. On busy days, it's a joy to pull out a meal and not have to cook.

It is an exciting challenge to learn as much as possible about being a homemaker. Psalm 101:2 says, "I will walk within my house with a perfect heart." Memorize that, and ask God that your house might have this kind of woman as its mistress.

PRIORITY #5—YOURSELF

You shall love your neighbor as yourself (Matt. 19:19).

Everyone needs time alone—time to read, to indulge in a hobby, or just to do nothing. Evaluate your weekly schedule and plan into it time for yourself. You will be a better functioning wife and mother if you have some time alone each week. As one dear woman in her fifties put it, "My husband finds me a much more interesting person when I have interests and activities that develop me as a person." God wants to develop you as a woman. Give Him some working time!

If you have children, the idea of having time to yourself may sound utterly impossible. Take heart! It is possible to do anything you really want to!

When I had small children, I traded off baby-sitting with a friend in the neighborhood. On Monday afternoon I took care of her two children for three hours, and then on Tuesday morning she had my three for three hours. I also participated in a neighborhood baby-sitting club; several young mothers baby-sat for each other, earning hours instead of money. Many women participate in a "mother's day out" program or hire a sitter. Whatever arrangements must be made, make them. You need and deserve a few hours each week to develop your creative abilities, to go shopping, or to do whatever you enjoy!

I remember years ago talking with the mother of teens who said her time alone was spent in bed on Monday morning, recuperating from the weekend. I thought then, *How strange. I'm sure I'll never do that!* As with so many other things, I have since eaten my words and discovered how nice a rest can be on Monday morning! After a weekend of waiting up late for daughters bubbling with excitement about their latest boyfriends and flipping pancakes for the extra teens who often stay at our house, I love to spend Monday morning alone (even sometimes in bed, but don't tell anyone).

PRIORITY #6—OUTSIDE THE HOME

> Go therefore and make disciples of all the nations (Matt. 28:19).

I was sharing my excitement about the priorities of a woman's life with a group of women in upstate New York, and one woman said, "Linda, I cannot believe what you are saying. I know that you believe the Great Commission to go into the world and preach the gospel was given to women as well as to men, yet here you are saying that our service for Christ is at the end of the list. Since I became a Christian two years ago, my service for the Lord has been first!"

I smiled and told her I'd like to ask her husband how he liked that!

When my children were very young, I decided before

God to keep my priorities in the order I've just shared. I still re-evaluate where I spend my time and seek to keep God first, Jody second, the children third, my home fourth, me fifth, and my outside activities sixth. Many times this is very difficult. It is *easier* to teach a Bible study than to stay home with three sick children. I fail many times, but I always come back to the same priorities. It's hard to describe the joy and satisfaction of knowing you are where God wants you and you are doing exactly what He wishes you to do. When you go along with God, amazing things result!

SATISFACTION GUARANTEED

Once while we were in upstate New York, it snowed furiously. Jody was at a conference with the car, and I was home pregnant with our third child. I remember thinking, *Lord, I would love to talk to someone older than two.* Then I remembered Jody had driven to the conference with another man, and I decided to call the man's wife. I didn't know her, but I figured she might be lonely, too.

As we talked, I realized she didn't understand why her husband had left her alone and gone with Jody. She was confused about his new commitment to Christ. When I found out she had a car, I invited her and her son to dinner and to spend the night. As we sat in our living room that night, I had the privilege of sharing the good news of Jesus Christ and seeing her commit her life to Him. God showed me He can use me right where I am as I keep my priorities in order.

Later, when we moved to Philadelphia in 1971, I asked God to use me in the lives of women—to teach, to train, to share the good news of eternal life in Jesus

Christ. I had no idea how God would accomplish that prayer! I had no car, I had one friend, and I had three little children. Not the most perfect combination to reach out to others! However, through my friend I met two other women, shared with them how to have evangelistic coffees, and began Bible study groups. As I began this project, I decided to be out of my home one to two mornings a week.

Throughout the year I kept my commitment, and I was overwhelmed by what God accomplished. Five Bible study groups were started, several women were trained, and many accepted Christ as their personal Savior. More was accomplished in that one year when I was out two mornings a week than when I had spent all my time ministering to women before I had children! Once again God blessed my ministry, because I was where He wanted me. My outreach was multiplied when I kept my priorities in order.

VARIETY IS THE SPICE OF LIFE

Each woman is different; each has varying responsibilities. One woman may have energy overflowing, while another begins to droop by four in the afternoon. As one friend put it, "Some women can run three-ring circuses, some two-ring, and some one-ring." It isn't important how many rings you can run. What is important is that before God you know yourself, your talents, and your emotional, spiritual, and physical capacities. "For I say, through the grace given to me, to everyone who is among you, not to think of himself more highly than he ought to think, but to think soberly, as God has dealt to each one a measure of faith" (Rom. 12:3).

You do not need to do everything your neighbor does. You are not your neighbor; you are you!

I know at this time in my life just how much I can handle outside my home and still be the wife and mother I want to be. I need to be home more now that our children are teenagers than I did when they were younger. If I'm gone all day long, racing in the door as the hungry teens invade the kitchen, I lack the physical, emotional, and spiritual energy to hold down the fort and be a patient, loving Mom until the last teen turns off his or her tape recorder! In a few years, I will be able to do more. Each of us needs to honestly evaluate and plan, according to our particular capacities and our set of circumstances.

WORKING WIVES

I can just hear some of you who work at a job outside the home saying, "All of this is fine and good for you full-time homemakers, but it won't work for me!" Yes, it will. If you work, your work is priority #6. You will not be able to spend the same quantity of time with your husband and children, or on your home, but the quality of time can be just the same. If you work, you should be even more organized than the full-time homemaker—make dinners on the weekends, get up early to get everything in order, and so on. You can still plan candlelight dinners for your husband and do many of the things I've shared. Sometimes a homemaker uses her children as an excuse for her lack of creativity, and a working woman uses her job as an excuse. In each case it takes much creativity, hard work, and perseverance, but it is worth it! Your attitude is the key. Do your husband and children feel they are most important, or do they feel you are "in love" with your work? I'm not saying it's easy. I'm saying it is well worth the effort!

PITFALLS

Before I end this discussion about priorities, I must warn about four potential problem areas.

1. A woman may forget Priority #1. *Activity* for God is substituted for a *relationship* with Him.
2. A woman may put her children before her husband. Consciously or unconsciously in word or in deed, she may put her children's wants and needs before those of her husband.
3. A woman may not keep her outside activities as Priority #6.
4. A woman may fail to realize that as the years pass the emphasis put in different priority areas will change. She needs to *constantly* re-evaluate her priority list.

A LIFE THAT COUNTS

I have a friend who is a missionary with her husband and children in Latin America. On a vacation, she was bitten by a scorpion and lay near death for two days. When she knew she would live, she wrote down some of the thoughts she had had as she lay dying:

> If it ends now for me, I wish it would have counted for more. But immediately I thought, *That is so foolish. It has counted with my husband and children where God has given me the most, along with the*

most responsibility. That is not to say my life was perfect or couldn't have been more, but it seemed God was saying to me, "Do not be a child, thinking those thoughts. You have counted where I have put you!"

My Own Robert Redford

One woman, when asked the difference between infatuation and love, answered:

> Infatuation is when you think that he's as sexy as Robert Redford, as smart as Henry Kissinger, as noble as Ralph Nader, as funny as Woody Allen, and as athletic as Jimmy Conners. Love is when you realize that he's as sexy as Woody Allen, as smart as Jimmy Conners, as funny as Ralph Nader, as athletic as Henry Kissinger, and nothing like Robert Redford—but you'll take him anyway![1]

Acceptance is taking him just as he is—strengths and weaknesses. What is God's view of partner acceptance, and what has He said about it? There are two commands given to a wife, both found in Ephesians 5. The first is to reverence her husband, and the second is to be submissive to him.

We'll take the easier first and start with reverence! The Greek word for *reverence* means "to be afraid of" or "to fear," "to be in awe of someone" or "to respect deeply." Sarah called Abraham lord. What does that mean today? Are you to call your husband lord, say, "Yes, sir," and bow or curtsy to him? Perhaps some husbands wouldn't think that was such a bad idea!

In the Amplified Bible, Ephesians 5:33 is translated, "And let the wife see that she respects and reverences her husband—that she notices him, regards him, honors him, prefers him, venerates and esteems him; and that she defers to him, praises him, and loves and admires him exceedingly!"

This passage makes it clear that a wife is to reverence her husband, but she may feel it is her God-ordained responsibility to revamp him! She may feel that getting a husband is like buying an old house. She sees it not the way it is but the way it's going to be when she gets it remodeled!

A wife may be so wrapped up in the negative aspects of her husband that she ignores the positive, but *reverence* is a positive word. It's an active verb. To reverence someone means to show admiration and respect for that person. Perhaps the thought of admiring and honoring her husband is foreign to a wife, maybe even repulsive. Certainly a wife who will not accept her husband as he is cannot reverence him. Before a wife can talk about reverencing, admiring, and uplifting her husband, she must learn to accept him as he is—no strings attached.

In the early years of our marriage, Jody called me his personal Holy Spirit. Wasn't he fortunate! I was sent by God to convict him of sin, judgment, and righteousness. I was sent to instruct him in proper etiquette, apparel, and personal habits, but it didn't work.

Each of us is human, and each of us has faults. When someone lives with another person day after day, it is easy to become irritated with that person's faults, and even to become obsessed with them. When asked to distinguish *love* from *like,* one man answered, "Love is the same as *like* except you feel sexier and more romantic. And also more annoyed when he talks with his mouth full. And resent it more when he interrupts you. And you also respect him less when he shows any weakness."

Many areas in my life need changing, and many areas in my husband's life need work. I'm sure the same is true for you and your husband as well! How do we change? How do we cause our husbands to change?

A wife can try being a personal Holy Spirit. She can try nagging, belittling, suggesting, advising until she faints from exhaustion. This is usually the human way of pursuing change.

THE HUMAN WAY OF EFFECTING CHANGE

It's easy for a wife to talk herself into trying to change her husband instead of allowing God His way. Why does a wife want her husband to change? Let's honestly examine these motivations.

1. *Because his habits are irritating.* Saturday morning rolls around and the wife is up at seven, sleepily pouring cereal into the bowls and realizing that Saturday is no different from any other day. How she'd like to sleep (especially when Happy Harry is snoring away)! As the clock reaches nine, then ten, her irritation grows. She slams doors, finds reasons to go into the bedroom, and makes snide remarks about hoping lover boy is enjoying his rest; then she goes back into the other room and fumes.

One husband's irritating habit was his erratic bath time. Here are his wife's comments:

At one time I was uptight about the time of day my husband took his bath! He got up, dressed, ate breakfast, read the paper, and then undressed and bathed. Imagine wasting all that time by dressing twice! I suggested, reasoned, nagged, pleaded, and ridiculed until we both felt our marriage balanced precariously on his bath time! Months passed before I realized that he had to get up earlier to compensate for wasted time. He worked hard enough to earn the right to "waste time" however he wanted. Furthermore, he heads this house; therefore he has freedom to bathe any hour of the day or night he chooses. (I still think it's silly, but I keep my opinion to myself. At 42, he should be old enough to know when to bathe.)[2]

2. *Because of a self-righteous attitude.* Doris was so holy she went to church every time the door was open. Each time, she reminded Larry that he should go, that he needed to go. And every time she said it, he decided again to stay home.

3. *For his benefit.* Sherry deeply loved her husband, all 250 pounds of him! His weight problem bothered her because she just knew he would have a heart attack at age forty or become diabetic if he didn't get that weight off. She constantly nagged Chuck to lose weight, and she tried everything to make him do it. The more she nagged, the more he ate. She would prepare low-calorie meals, but he would eat what he wanted in secret. Her desire for him to change stemmed from a sincere motive, but it still didn't work!

4. *What will people think?* Sue really does love her husband and she is convinced if he would dress in some of the "in" styles, instead of that old double-

breasted jacket he wears so often, he would be more highly thought of by others.

Every wife wants her husband to be liked and accepted by her family, and I was no exception! My family lives on the beach in southern California, and to them, heaven is spending an entire day lying on the sand doing nothing. My dear husband does not know how to "do nothing." On our trips to California, he always took his books so that while the family was basking in the sun and enjoying the sand and surf, Jody was in the house reading Athanasius' *Exposition of the Hypostatic Union.* I was sure my family would think that very odd, so I went to work being his personal Holy Spirit!

"Honey, don't you like the sun? It really is nice" . . . *ad nauseum.* Jody continued to read, and I continued to suspect that my family was convinced I'd married a weirdo. (Of course, they felt no such thing.)

God finally succeeded in getting me to accept Jody just as he is, a wonderful individual created by God for a special purpose. When I allowed Jody the freedom to be what he is, a scholar, he reciprocated by trying to be all I desired.

Not long after one of our California visits, he returned for a speaking engagement and visited my family. He wrote me from their home: "Dear Honey. Would you believe in one day I have gone on a boat ride, lain in the sun, ridden a bike, walked to the fun zone, and gone swimming? I am the well-rounded all-American boy!"

5. *For the sake of the children.* A wife's heartfelt motivation behind wanting her husband to have nice table manners is to set an example for the children. Is

that so wrong? What about the church elder who swears at home in front of the children, and they see what a hypocrite he is. Shouldn't a wife see that he changes his ways?

We've looked at some motivations for forcing a husband to change. Now let's look at some of the areas in his life that a wife may try to change.

AREAS FOR CHANGE[3]

1. *His personal habits.* Perhaps it's the way he hangs up his towel (in a pile on the bathroom floor), or maybe it's his violent temper tantrums.

Paula's husband had a drinking problem. As the drinking increased, so did his time away from home. Night after night he would come in early in the morning smelling of liquor and the perfume of other women. Paula threatened, screamed, and cried, but to no avail.

When she became a Christian, she asked God to enable her to love her husband just as he was. I'm sure you'll agree that was no small task! Paula quit belittling her husband before the children. When they asked where he was, she simply said that he was with his friends. When she heard him stumble in at three in the morning, she got up and told him she had prepared his favorite dinner and would like to get it for him.

The poor man was stupefied. Paula continued to give, and by Christmas her husband said with tears in his eyes, "I wish I could give you a sober husband by Christmas, but I can't."

It would be a nice fairy tale if I told you that one week later he changed. It wasn't one week. It was more like one year, during which time Paula continued to suffer. Recently Paula communicated to a friend that the changes in their home were remarkable. She said her husband had stopped drinking and had accepted Christ as his Savior, and the family members were happier than they had ever been.

2. *His attitude toward the children.* One wife would like to see her husband spend more time with the children. Another would like her husband to set up regular devotional times with the children. Still another wife would just like her husband to be home long enough to confirm the rumor that the children do actually have a father!

3. *His handling of the finances.* A wife longs for her husband to be financially responsible. I know a wife who has hidden money and the checkbook from her husband and has kept a secret bank account. Another wife doles out an allowance to her husband as if he were a little boy. When a husband is irresponsible with money, his wife becomes increasingly insecure, and insecurity is crippling to a marriage.

4. *Sex life.* One woman put the problem very well when she said, "I'm tired of Harry's Neanderthal approach to sex. After the ten o'clock news, he says in a monotone, 'You wanna do it?'"

5. *His lack of spiritual leadership.* In the early years of our marriage, we belonged to a wonderful church. Because I was Jody's personal Holy Spirit, it was important to me that he be well thought of. Jody doesn't like to sing, and during church he would stand like a toy soldier staring off into space while everyone was singing. I was afraid people would think he was disinterested because of his lack of involvement.

So I swooped into action, nudging him, whispering

in his ear that he should sing, and later giving him a lengthy discourse on the merits of singing in church. Of course this didn't change Jody. It only resulted in a quarrel on the way home. It embarrasses me that I nagged and quarreled about such a relatively insignificant thing. Nagging will not produce a spiritual giant. Only God the Holy Spirit can do that!

6. *His social habits.* I have a friend, Joan, who is from a wealthy family in Saint Louis. While a student, Joan fell in love with a West Texas farmboy. (He wasn't really a hick, but then not exactly what you'd find in high society either!) As happens with engaged couples, Joan and Steve went to Saint Louis for a party given by her relatives. Everyone wanted to meet her fiancé!

The meal was lovely, with roast beef, potatoes, and delicious gravy. Steve had a piece of roll and some gravy left, so he did what every self-respecting West Texan would do: he sopped up the gravy with his bread! Watching in horror, Joan surreptitiously took her salad fork and jabbed it into his leg under the table. Steve was furious and didn't say another word during the dinner. Joan said her relatives thought he had little personality because he was so quiet. But she knew!

7. *His aspirations.* One husband may work himself into a heart attack, but another husband may seem to have no ambition whatever. One wife told me she knew her husband could become president of the company, but he had no desire to do it. He was perfectly content where he was. She had other plans for him, however, and the inevitable quarrels resulted.

8. *His household duties.* The garbage, the light bulbs, the outdoor Christmas tree lights! At our house, the Christmas lights came down on March 17 one year! I

was beginning to think it might be good to just leave them up until next year. Plenty of wives have gripes about male procrastination.

9. *His time at home.* Perhaps a wife feels slighted because her husband spends so much time at his office or on the golf course or with the "boys." One wife tried nagging, crying, screaming, and everything she could think of to make her husband see that she needed him home before 10:00 P.M. Finally she decided to change her tactics. She began to do things like taking dinner to his office and writing him love notes. He began staying home more—and liking it!

RESULTS

We've seen some of the motivations and rationalizations behind wanting a husband to change. We've seen some of the areas in his life a wife may try to change. Now let's look at the results of a wife's trying to revamp a husband her way.

1. *Tension.* Even when a husband and a wife truly love each other, the fierce competition of wills causes marital tension, which invariably erupts in disastrous ways.

2. *Destruction of love.* When a woman tries to change a man, she pits herself against him. A husband may stop loving his wife if she consistently acts like a combination mother, spiritual adviser, and dietitian.

3. *Rebellion.* Most men like to come up with the ideas. If a wife nags her husband to diet, for instance, very likely he will rebel. He knows he needs to diet, but he will fight the attempt to run his life.

4. *Discouragement.* It's a wife's job to make her hus-

band whole: it's God's responsibility to make him holy. Isn't that fantastic! God gave a wife to a husband to love him, to build him up, and to make him happy. God the Holy Spirit does not need a wife to be a personal Holy Spirit. He will work alone to bring about the needed changes in lives. God has a special and unique plan for each individual and each marriage. His timing may not be human timing, but be assured that He is at work.

Believe me, the human way of getting change doesn't work. God, on the other hand, guarantees results. Why not take a few tips from Him?

GOD'S WAY OF EFFECTING CHANGE

Step 1. *Learn to totally accept your husband.*

If you want to win the deep love of your husband, you must be satisfied with his total person as he exists now. You prove your acceptance of him by not trying to change him.

I can hear you saying, "That is humanly impossible." You're right!

The basis of partner acceptance is the cross of Jesus Christ. Until we have been totally forgiven, we cannot forgive. *Until we have been totally loved and accepted, we cannot love and accept our husbands.*

I'd like to share with you how God brought me to a point where I was able to begin to forgive, to love unconditionally, and to accept my husband and others just as they are—with no condition of change.

As a young girl I was labeled the all-American girl. I tried hard and usually attained whatever I aimed for in life. I figured that at the end of my life God would weigh my good works against my bad; if the good works tipped the scale, I'd be in! Then, as a teenager I came up against a problem for which I had no solution. My father was an alcoholic, and during my growing-up years, I had grown to resent him. He had torn our family apart and had terribly hurt my mother, brother, and me; I found it very difficult to forgive and accept him.

Although my wonderful mother provided stability in the midst of suffering, I had insecurities, and they manifested themselves in my relationships with boys. From junior high school on, I always had a boyfriend! A class ring, a fraternity pin, a commitment to marry, and yet the relationships never lasted. I was the fickle of the fickle! Deep down I was afraid that when I married, I would be happy for six months and then find someone who looked better. This had been the pattern for so many years, I questioned whether I could love with a lasting and committed love.

As a college student I was invited to hear a speaker talk about the claims of Jesus Christ. I went because I was religious, and besides, I was interested in the boy who had invited me. That night I heard for the first time that Christianity is not a list of rules, it is not an ethical code or a philosophy of life. It is a relationship— a relationship with Jesus Christ. And I learned that I could enter into this relationship by realizing that I needed Christ, that I could not earn my way to heaven by my good life, by my sincere efforts, or by my religious activity.

Never had I been willing to admit that I was sinful. Sin was murder and adultery, and besides, I tried hard. Sincerity had to count for something.

Through God's Word I realized that sin is not just

deeds but attitudes—an attitude of indifference or independence of God—and that my sins or selfishness separated me from God. Christ was the only One who could forgive my sin.

A story put it into focus for me. Suppose while driving down a street, a woman named Gail received a speeding ticket and was summoned to appear in court. As she stood before the judge, she was declared guilty, and the sentence was fifty dollars or five days. Meekly she began to open her checkbook, but just then the judge stood up and took off his robe. Gail saw to her astonishment that it was her father! He came toward her and said, "Gail, you're guilty. You've transgressed the law, and you deserve to pay the penalty. But because I love you, I want to pay it for you." With that, he pulled out *his* checkbook and wrote a check for fifty dollars.

This is a picture of exactly what God, our Father, did when Jesus died on the cross. God, the righteous Judge, declared us guilty of sin, but as our loving Father He did not want us to have to pay the penalty of eternal death and separation from Him. God sent His only Son to die so that you and I might be forgiven and have eternal life. When Jesus Christ uttered His final words from the cross, "It is finished," or literally from the Greek, "Paid in full," He was paying my penalty and yours just as the judge in the story.

The penalty had been paid, but Gail still had to make a decision. Would she be a rebellious child and defiantly say, "Thanks but no thanks. You can keep your check. I'll do it myself"? Or would she reach out and gratefully accept the gift offered in love? This story helped me slowly realize that I personally needed to reach out and accept God's gift.

For twenty years I had been trying to grow and yet had not been born spiritually. One day I quietly locked the door, pulled down the shades (God forbid that anyone should see me!), and told God I was a fake—I'd gone through all the religious motions and called myself a Christian, never knowing who Jesus Christ really is and what He has done for me. Very simply I prayed, telling God of my need, thanking Him for sending Christ to die for me on the cross, and asking Christ to come into my life, forgive my sins, and make me into the kind of woman He wanted me to be. I knew that God had totally forgiven me and that He totally loved and accepted me.

As I continued to grow in His love, I was able to go to my father and forgive him and love him just as he was. I also knew I was able to make a commitment to love someone else as God had loved me, unconditionally with no strings attached. If you have never received Christ as your Savior and Lord, you can change your eternal destiny now by quietly putting down this book and inviting Christ to come into your life and forgive your sins.

God's grace is the foundation of partner acceptance. I personally believe it is very difficult, if not impossible, to accept your husband unless you have experienced God's forgiveness and acceptance yourself. Now that you understand Step 1, God's love and acceptance, you're ready to go on to Step 2, applying this concept to your husband.

Step 2. *Get rid of the plank in your own eye.*

And why do you look at the speck in your brother's eye, but do not consider the plank in your own eye?

Or how can you say to your brother, "Let me remove the speck out of your eye"; and look, a plank is in your own eye? Hypocrite! First remove the plank from your own eye, and then you will see clearly to remove the speck out of your brother's eye (Matt. 7:3–5).

Often a wife is so concerned with her husband's faults that she cannot see her own! Jay Adams begins his marriage counseling with the following project (see sample next page). In the left-hand column, a wife lists all her mate's faults. Then in the right-hand column, she lists seventy-five of her wrong responses to those faults. Perhaps her husband's fault is that he is messy. What is her response? Does she nag, sigh, scream, give him the silent treatment, or throw the clothes he leaves lying around?

I encourage you to do this exercise. Do it now. Get out a piece of paper and make your columns. List your husband's faults and as many of your wrong responses as you can think of. You'll be surprised that your responses are as bad or worse than his faults. After you have finished, confess your wrong attitudes to God and burn the paper. Definitely *do not* show it to your husband. This exercise is for your benefit—to help you get the plank out of your own eye!

PLANK REMOVAL

Faults	Wrong Responses
1. Lack of time spent with children	1. Nag
	2. Belittle
	3. Sigh and moan
	4. Compare with other men
	5. Criticize
	6. Neglect
	7. Reject as person
	8. Cool sexually
	9. Anger
	10. Indifference
	11. Gossip to other women
	12. Publicly tear him down
	13. Quote Bible verses
	14. Feel self-righteous
	15. Feel bitter
	16. Silence

Step 3. *Give your rights to God.*

One wife may feel that her husband should meet all her needs for love, affection, friendship, security, and so on. Another wife may feel that because she has worked hard on her marriage she deserves to have a perfect husband.

Ruth Graham, wife of Billy Graham, makes the following statement:

> I pity the married couple who expect too much from one another. It is a foolish woman who expects her husband to be to her that which only Jesus Christ can be: always ready to forgive, totally understanding, unendingly patient, invariably tender and loving,

unfailing in every area, anticipating every need, and
making more than adequate provision. Such expectations put a man under an impossible strain.[4]

We must be realistic and not expect our husbands
to be what only God can be to us or to be something
totally alien to their personality and temperament. Our
expectations are a key barrier to accepting our husbands
at face value. To get rid of your expectations, you must
lay aside what you feel you deserve in a husband.

Paul said, "In humility consider others better than
yourselves" (Phil. 2:3 NIV), and "others" includes husbands. "Your attitude should be the same as that of
Christ Jesus: who, being in very nature God, did not
consider equality with God something to be grasped"
(Phil. 2:5–6 NIV). Christ was God and deserved all of
the rights of Deity. He didn't regard equality with God
a thing to be grasped. He didn't consider His rights as
an equal with God something He should cling to. If
Jesus didn't cling to His "rights" as Deity, then we
should follow His example. Lay aside what you think
you *deserve* in a husband and give up your expectations
of change. Look at what Christ did. He "made himself
nothing, taking the very nature of a servant, being made
in human likeness" (Phil. 2:7 NIV). He emptied Himself,
laying aside the rights of Deity. His focus became serving
others rather than serving Himself.

Too often a wife's focus is on getting her husband
to change to suit her—not for his benefit but for hers.
Paul advised the Philippians: "Do nothing out of selfish
ambition or vain conceit" (Phil. 2:3 NIV). Many times
the desire to change a husband springs from selfish
motives because a wife's real focus is on herself.

What was Christ's reward? Was it praise from men?

No. It was praise from God! "Therefore God also has highly exalted Him and given Him the name which is above every name" (Phil. 2:9). Because Christ laid aside all His rights so that He could do God's will and because He adopted a servant's heart, God has highly exalted Him. His reward was from God.

One woman protested, "I tried this before for two weeks. I gave up all my rights, and my husband still didn't change."

The reward she wanted was a changed husband. The reward she should have been seeking was praise from God. She should do this not because of what she is going to get but because she is being a faithful servant. Instead of demanding a certain kind of husband, she should give up her rights to God. When she receives a loving or tender or understanding husband, she should see him as a gift from God and not as a "right."

On the next page there is a list of the nine areas you might like to see changed in your husband. Copy the chart on page 101 on a sheet of paper and fill in what you have wanted changed in each area. Add others if you like. Now copy the words of Philippians 2:5–7 over the chart and throw it away. Once you have given up your rights to everything you feel you deserve in a husband, you will be free to emphasize the positive.

Step 4. *Discern positive qualities.*

> Finally, brethren, whatever things are true, whatever things are noble, whatever things are just, whatever things are pure, whatever things are lovely, whatever things are of good report, if there is any virtue and if there is anything praiseworthy— meditate on these things (Phil. 4:8).

GIVE YOUR RIGHTS TO GOD

Category of Expectation	Desired Change ("My Rights")
1. Personal habits	A neat husband who *always* hangs towels and clothes and puts away shoes!
2. Children	A husband who takes a *deep* interest in everything the children do, disciplines, instructs, and plays with the children!
3. Finances	A husband who is financially responsible, pays bills on time, and gives me *lots* of extra money!
4. Sex	A husband who is *very* romantic, tender, exciting, sensitive, and loving!
5. Spiritual	
6. Social	
7. Aspirations	
8. Duties	
9. Time	

Does your husband get up and go to work each day? Thank God for this. Does he want to be a man of God? Thank God for this. Does he play with the children? Thank God for this.

In fact, why don't you thank God for everything positive about him? Take out another sheet of paper, and write down all the things you have to be thankful for about your husband. You don't need to tear this one up; in fact, you can show it to him!

Step 5. *Ask your husband's forgiveness.*

So if you are standing before the altar in the Temple, offering a sacrifice to God, and suddenly remember that a friend has something against you, leave your sacrifice there beside the altar and go and apologize and be reconciled to him, and then come and offer your sacrifice to God (Matt. 5:23–24 TLB).

A wife may have totally alienated her husband through her failure to accept him. She may have wounded his male ego so deeply that she has caused him to rebel against her. In such a situation, a wife needs to ask her husband's forgiveness.

Before you can begin building your marriage, before you can reverence and submit to your husband, you need to seek his forgiveness for your wrong attitudes. Do not do this hastily as an emotional gesture because of reading this book. Think about it, pray about it, and ask God's wisdom concerning whether you should ask his forgiveness, and if so, how you should ask it.

If after much prayer and thought you feel the need to clean the slate and admit your wrong to your husband, approach him in such a way that *all the blame is cast on you.* For instance, do not say, "Honey, because you've been such a hard person to live with and because of your many bad habits, I have not been a good wife." Remember, you are asking forgiveness, not telling him his faults!

Perhaps you could say something like this: "Honey, I've recently realized that I have not loved you as I should, and I want to ask your forgiveness." Or "Honey, I know that I have not been considerate of your feelings, and I want to ask you to forgive me." Then ask him, "Will you forgive me?"

Many of you will feel no need to ask forgiveness. You can go right on to the positive. But for others, the dirt must be removed from the glass before it can be filled with clean, fresh water.

Step 6. *Verbalize your acceptance.*

That is what the next chapter is about! Reverence is putting your total acceptance into practice. Once you accept your husband as he is with no condition of change, you are ready to begin to notice him, regard him, honor him, prefer him, venerate and esteem him, praise and love and admire him exceedingly!

6

His Greatest Fan

He began his life with all the classic handicaps and disadvantages. His mother was a powerfully built, domineering woman who found it difficult to love anyone. She had been married three times, and her second husband divorced her because she beat him up regularly. The father of the child I'm describing was her third husband; he died of a heart attack a few months before the child's birth. As a consequence, the mother had to work long hours from his earliest childhood. She gave him no affection, no love, no discipline, and no training during those early years. She even forbade him to call her at work. Other children had little to do with him, so he was alone most of the time. He was absolutely rejected from his earliest childhood. He was ugly and poor and untrained and unlovable. When he was thirteen years old a school psychologist commented that he probably didn't even know the meaning of the word "love." During adolescence, the girls would have nothing to do with him and he fought with the boys. Despite a high IQ, he failed academically, and finally dropped out during his third year of high school. He thought he might find a new acceptance in the Marine Corps; they reportedly built men, and he wanted to be one. But his problems went with him. The other Marines laughed at him and ridiculed him.

He fought back, resisted authority, and was court-martialed and thrown out of the Marines with an undesirable discharge. So there he was—a young man in his early twenties—absolutely friendless and ship-wrecked. He was small and scrawny in stature. He had an adolescent squeak in his voice. He was bald-ing. He had no talent, no skill, no sense of worthiness. He didn't even have a driver's license. Once again he thought he could run from his problems so he went to live in a foreign country. But he was rejected there too. Nothing had changed. While there, he mar-ried a girl who herself had been an illegitimate child and brought her back to America with him. Soon, she began to develop the same contempt for him that everyone else displayed. She bore him two chil-dren, but he never enjoyed the status and respect that a father should have. His marriage continued to crumble. His wife demanded more and more things that he could not provide. Instead of being his ally against the bitter world, as he hoped, she became his most vicious opponent. She could outfight him, and she learned to bully him. On one occasion, she locked him in the bathroom as punishment. Finally, she forced him to leave. He tried to make it on his own but he was terribly lonely. After days of solitude, he went home and literally begged her to take him back. He surrendered all pride. He crawled. He ac-cepted humiliation. He came on her terms. Despite his meager salary, he brought her seventy-eight dol-lars as a gift, asking her to take it and spend it any way she wished. But she laughed at him. She belittled his feeble attempts to supply the family's needs. She ridiculed his failure. She made fun of his sexual impotency in front of a friend who was there. At one point, he fell on his knees and wept bitterly, as the greater darkness of his private nightmare enveloped him. Finally in silence, he pleaded no more. No one wanted him. No one had ever wanted him. He was perhaps the most rejected man of our time. His ego lay shattered in fragmented dust. The next day, he was a strangely different man. He arose, went to the garage and took down a rifle he had hidden there. He carried it with him to his newly acquired job at a book-storage building. And from a window on the third floor of that building, shortly after noon, Nov. 22, 1963, he sent two shells crashing into the head of President John Kennedy. Lee Harvey Oswald, the rejected, unlovable failure, killed the man who, more than any other man on earth, embodied all the success, beauty, wealth and family affection which he lacked. In firing that rifle, he utilized the one skill he had learned in his entire, miserable lifetime.[1]

When I first read this about Lee Harvey Oswald in the excellent book *Hide or Seek* by James Dobson, I was overwhelmed by the thoughts: *Would the story have been different if his wife had been his ally against the cruel world instead of his most bitter opponent? Could he have slowly but surely grown into a mature man if his wife had stood behind him, been on his team, and admired him?*

Psychiatrists say a man's most basic needs, apart from warm sexual love, are approval and admiration. In our society there is an epidemic of inferiority. Many times marriage problems are essentially personal problems, and often the personal problems are related to a bad self-image. Many of the problems in our society are due to the fact that men will not be men. They will not assume leadership. The reason they refuse to take the lead is often due to deep-seated fears and insecurities. Because this occurs at an emotional level, it is often difficult to express.

The word *reverence* means "to stand in awe of," which encompasses "to respect, honor, esteem, adore, praise, enjoy, and admire." Admiration is one major thing a wife can do to build up her husband's self-image. Even if your husband already has a healthy view of himself, *God can use your admiration to build him into more of the man God wants him to be* and into the husband you want him to be!

Your husband's self-image is directly connected to your private and public admiration and praise. It has been said, "Behind every great man there is a great woman." I feel a great wife is one who would admire, build up, and glorify her husband, thus transforming and enhancing his image of himself. There are three key words to building your husband's self-image: (1) *accept* him at face value; (2) *admire* his manly qualities; and (3) submit to his *authority*.

YOUR PRIVATE LIFE

Do you build up or destroy? What do you communicate to your husband when he walks in the door after work? Genuine encouragement, or dissatisfaction? Does your face light up when he talks to you, or does he see sneers and a lack of trust? A man can have everything outside the home, but if the sincere respect of his wife and children is missing, he can be totally emasculated.

George was such a man. Anyone who knew him would laugh if you suggested he could ever be emasculated! George had everything. He had always excelled;

he had always been the best at everything he tried. After graduating from law school, he easily acquired a $100,000-a-year job. He was highly respected by his peers, by his employers, and by everyone in the business community. With athletic prowess, wealth, and success, what more could any man want?

The more George desperately wanted and needed was the respect and admiration of his wife. Instead of being his *creative counterpart*, she had set herself up to win the victory in their home. If he excelled, she would excel more. They each did their "own thing," but she was determined *her* "own thing" would be better than *his!* Gradually her attitude began to destroy him emotionally. Distracted and unhappy, he lost his job.

In desperation, George agreed to work with his wife to write a book on modern marriage. The book sold more than 200,000 copies propagating the do-your-own-thing philosophy, yet their own marriage was in pathetic shape. His wife left him, and he went to work as a janitor.

Then a friend of ours met and shared the love of Jesus Christ with him. He responded and accepted Christ, and his life began to change. He saw for the first time what had happened in his marriage and why. He saw the roles God had given husbands and wives, and he realized his marriage had been a blasphemy.

George wrote a letter to his wife, asking her forgiveness for his failure to be the head of their home. He told her of his desire to have a renewed marriage in Christ. His marriage is not together yet, but with the encouragement of Christ, he has put his life together. He has acquired another lucrative job in the legal profession, making use of his capabilities, and he is on the road to being the man God wants him to be.

I hear you saying, "That is a pretty far-out example! From an executive to a janitor, all because of a woman!" Sure, it's far-out. Even though it doesn't always happen to this extreme, tragic things can and will happen when a wife fails to give her husband the reverence that God intended and that he desperately needs.

IN THE PUBLIC EYE

Just what does the public see? What image of your husband do others receive from you? God says you should be publishing his virtues, broadcasting your love and admiration for him by all you do and say. Do your neighbors and friends think your husband is a wonder or a slob? Where did they get their information?

In Proverb 31 we read, "Her husband is known in the gates, / When he sits among the elders of the land." One modern writer interpreted this: "Her husband is highly thought of by others because she never berates him."

A national sales executive came to New York City and put an ad in the paper with an offer to twenty men who would meet his qualifications. He offered $35,000 a year for five years plus $250,000 to $1 million to start their own businesses. He opened shop in a motel room for three weeks, interviewing men for eighteen hours a day. At the end of three weeks he had his twenty men.

Then he did a very unusual thing. He asked to interview the wives of the twenty men. One by one the women came, and after talking with all twenty women, he had only nine men left. He said he did not interview the women to determine their intelligence, their beauty, or their poise. He interviewed each woman to see if she was on her husband's team and would stand behind him. He said he was offering the men a great opportunity, but one that would require hard work and dedication. He knew that without the encouragement and praise of their wives the men would not succeed. Would your husband have been one of the nine men left?

It seems clear from Ephesians 5 that a wife is to admire her husband and build him up. Most of us know from experience that every man, woman, and child needs admiration. So why does a wife fail to give her husband the admiration he needs?

BARRIERS TO ADMIRATION

Feelings of awkwardness. Isn't it strange that a wife can admire a friend's hairdo, hanging plants, or Hungarian goulash, but she often cannot or will not express admiration to her husband? Maybe she is afraid it will embarrass him or make him feel awkward. Some people just don't know how to accept compliments, or give them.

Too self-centered already. I have heard this statement many times as a wife's reason for her lack of admiration. Perhaps her husband's egotism or boasting is a cry for admiration. No one else builds him up, so he has to.

No apparent admirable qualities. First Corinthians 13 says that love "believes all things" (v. 7). One woman, when told to express admiration toward her husband, said that there was simply nothing about him to admire. The teacher of the seminar asked her to go far back into their marriage and find something she had admired. Obediently the woman went home and told her husband she had admired the way he handled their money during the depression. (I call that really delving back!) The poor man, starved for admiration and appreciation, turned to his wife with tears in his eyes. He had been longing for that for over thirty years!

Goethe, the German author, said that if you treat a man as he is, he will stay as he is, but if you treat him as if he were what he ought to be, and could be, he will become the bigger and better man.

Jesus was a master at seeing people not as they were but as they could be. The apostle Peter was a perfect example. Peter the impulsive, Peter the anxious (he reminds me of me), was always ready to leap before looking. Jesus said to this impulsive fisherman, "Simon, you shall be Peter," meaning "the Rock" (see John 1:42). Now Peter was a lot of things, but one thing he was not was a rock. A marshmallow, perhaps, but never a rock! Jesus saw him, however, not as he was but as he would become. The Peter who denied Christ three times later became the leader of the early church and a man who was crucified because he would not deny his faith in Jesus.

Failure to accept him at face value. Until a wife totally accepts her husband with no condition of change, it will be very difficult for her to admire him. The negative must be removed before the positive can be planted.

DEVELOPING ADMIRATION

One of a kind. All men are *not* the same. Each is a separate individual. His hobby can run the gamut from wild game hunting to needlepoint. How well do you really know your husband? More and more I am impressed that God has given each man one woman who knows him intimately and can meet his needs. I don't need to know or understand my neighbor's husband or your husband—just my own. My husband is an individual, unlike any other man, and I am to discover him.

The questions on the next page are a tool to help you in learning to discover your husband. I encourage you to write the answers to the questions on a sheet of paper. Then tonight ask your husband the questions and see how well you did!

Several years ago I asked my husband similar questions and found out I didn't know him nearly as well as I thought. I asked him to list some of his happiest times. He remembered a three-hour discussion we had in upstate New York, in which he felt we communicated in a fantastic way. When I said, "What discussion?" he could not believe I didn't remember!

His second answer was, "My first day at seminary." It was my turn to be flabbergasted. (It was then that I knew we would be returning to seminary for his doctorate!) I had been with him at seminary for four long years and had not grasped the significance of this experience in his life.

During the two-day seminar I give, "How to Be a Creative Counterpart," I ask the women to answer these questions and then ask their husbands for their answers. Amazing things have resulted. One woman wrote me the following note:

> Last night I did what you asked us to. When we got to the question about his deepest fears in life, he began to open up and shared for the first time in our thirty years of marriage his fears about his business. We talked and cried together for three hours, and I'm convinced it was the beginning of a new marriage relationship for us.

DO YOU REALLY KNOW YOUR HUSBAND?

1. What is the happiest thing that has ever happened to your husband?

2. What has been the hardest experience of his life?

3. What are his secret ambitions, his goals for life?

4. What are his deep fears?

5. What about you does he appreciate the most?

6. What traits of yours would he like to see changed?

7. What man or men does he most admire?

The first suggestion for discovering your husband has been to communicate with him. Too many married couples talk about trivia and never really get inside their partners to discover the joys, hurts, successes, and failures.

Wild game hunting or needlepoint? Take an interest in your husband's interests. That may sound easy, but for some of us it's not! My husband is interested in deep theological study, astrophysics, computers, Greek exegesis, evolution–creation, and jogging. Jody tried unsuccessfully for nine years to get me out on the track. I had many good excuses: it was hot; I would perspire and ruin my hairdo; I couldn't make it around the track; I had too many things to do. One night he took my resting heartbeat, and it was eighty. Then he took his, and it was fifty-seven. He explained to me that my heart was beating 33,120 times a day more than his, and thus I was wearing out faster.

That did it! I was off to the track! I learned much about my husband and found many new things to admire about him. He has a fantastic build, and besides that, how many men can run five miles every day? (My appreciation climbed when I discovered how hard it was to run one mile, let alone five!) It has also been good for my figure. Jody is concerned about my heart. I'm concerned about my hips. Jogging helps both!

After we moved to Austria, skiing became the family sport. Jody was already a great skier, and the kids caught on immediately. I was a slow learner because I had to first get over my fear of the chair lift before I could begin to ski. (I've decided that nothing is easy to learn after age thirty-five—especially skiing and a second language, and I've struggled to do both!) But I'm glad I persevered! Jody and I ski together, stopping at Alpine huts on the way down the hill to sip hot chocolate and talk.

I have a dear friend whose husband is an avid fisherman. When they were newly married, he suggested they go fishing. Because she had heard that the family that plays together, stays together, she went. She recounted that the first time she put a minnow on a fishing hook, she was sure she would vomit. As with most things, it got easier, and soon she could do it without closing her eyes.

Now, many years and four children later, she is thankful she became interested in her husband's interests. She recently said, "Linda, do you know the best time Bruce and I had last year? It was at 6:00 A.M. cleaning fish by the lake. The children were asleep, and we talked of deep and wonderful things we rarely talk about as we cleaned the fish. I thanked God that morning that I had been willing to put that first minnow on the hook."

Are you listening? Can your husband talk to you and not be ridiculed? Can he confide in you and know his confidences will be safely guarded? Do you minimize his weaknesses and emphasize his manliness and his strengths? Do you create a climate in which he feels safe to voice his fears because you believe in him? Do you treat your husband as the most special person in the world, or are you more polite to the neighbors? You teach your children to be polite, yet how polite are you to their father?

If a wife collapses on the couch, completely exhausted from a hard day, her husband is supposed to be understanding, isn't he? Yet let an insurance salesperson or a friend drop by, and she is instant smiles, coffee, and conversation! I'm not saying a wife should never "let her hair down" with her husband, but she may let it down and never roll it up again!

Sometimes a wife complains that her husband won't talk to her, but perhaps she fails to encourage him to talk. Often when talking to Jody, I sit with my yarn in my lap and crochet. One night he said, "Honey, I'm tired of talking to your crochet hook! Do you have any idea how distracting it is to talk to someone whose hands are always moving ninety miles an hour?"

Draw him out. Set aside time each day to talk to him. Often I take an index card and write down all Jody is doing that day. As I pray for him, I refer to the card and feel as if I'm vitally involved in each thing he does. At the end of the day, I am full of pertinent questions.

We have found that we talk better away from home. This may not be true for you. We love our home, but there are always interruptions: two phones ringing, children needing attention, persons delivering packages, and many more. On our "dates," we go to a restaurant and sit and talk. We always find that we talk on a deeper level and communicate better away from the distractions of home. This technique may not appeal to you and your husband, so find something that works for you and do it!

If a husband is in a highly scientific or intellectually abstract profession, his wife may say it is difficult to communicate with him about his work. I can sympathize. Many of Jody's abstract theological concepts are real mind blowers! I find that when I'm really interested, however, I can understand almost anything. That's the key. I can also notice how absorbed he is in his subject, how he has mastered the intricate details, how he has worked out and developed his ideas, and how loyal to them he is. Even when I can't totally understand all he is saying, I can look for character traits to admire.

Don't interrupt. This sounds simple, but you may be guilty here. He begins, and you finish the sentence for him. After all, you know him so well that you are sure you know just what he is going to say. At other times, you may be so wrapped up in what you want to say that you rudely interrupt to get your ideas across. Does this sound familiar?

Learning to accept your husband's feelings, tastes, and attitudes can go a long way toward establishing the kind of good communication we talk so much about. Does it matter whether acorn squash is good for him if he doesn't like it? Accept his tastes. He doesn't need a dietitian or a substitute mother. Maybe he gets a kick out of football, and you feel the sport is stupid. Voice that opinion once or twice, and what will you communicate? That you feel you married a stupid man. How willing do you think he'll be to express his likes and dislikes if he is called stupid when he does?

Forget the past. John comes home and says he has a fantastic land deal and is going to invest. Becky hysterically reminds him that their last real estate investment was a total and complete flop. "How can you think of doing it again? Don't you love me?" End of communication. John stomps into the other room and slams the door.

It's normal for a wife to have fears in an area in which her husband has failed before, but how much better to have handled it like this: John says he has a fantastic land deal. Becky says, "Tell me more about it, John. It sounds exciting!" Beginning of conversation. John opens up and shares, and Becky comments and asks more questions. She tells John she's happy he's found property he feels so good about.

Later she says, "You know, John, it's wonderful to have a husband I can lean on and trust. I know we both remember well the last investment fiasco, but I know you'll check into this one thoroughly. And I have confidence in your decision." Wow! This time John spends hours investigating the property. Why? Because he wants to live up to what Becky feels he is!

Let him dream. A wife may tramp through her marriage with hobnail boots, stepping on each and every dream. My husband said unexpectedly one night, "I'd like to go to Mount Ararat and look for Noah's Ark." Immediately, (practical woman that I am) I had to remind him that it would be terribly expensive, impossible for the children, and ridiculous for anyone but a professional climber.

A man likes to dream. He may say, "Wouldn't it be fun to own a boat?" or "Let's take our savings and go around the world." Then a practical wife fills in the reasons why it's impossible. The tragedy is not that a husband dreams the impossible dream but that he quits dreaming altogether thanks to a "practical" wife.

If you know your husband's dreams, you'll come a long way toward knowing him. If he feels free to express his dreams, you'll become more aware of him and his admirable qualities. Sometimes he just wants to bounce his ideas off someone. Does he feel free to do it with you, or does he go to a business associate or another woman?

Have you ever considered how Sarah must have felt when Abraham decided to trade his mansion for a tent and go find a new land in a place he didn't know?

How do you suppose Mrs. Noah felt when Noah shared his dream of a big boat he wanted to build in the middle of the desert? It had never rained before on earth, and her husband wanted to build an ark for the coming flood!

How about Job's wife? What an encouragement she was! Totally defeated, physically ill, Job was trying to believe God and find the meaning in his suffering. In came his wife, who said, "Curse God and die!" (Job 2:9). Who needs encouragement like that?

An added tip from Jody: don't say "always" and "never." "But, Honey, you *never* do that when I want you to." Or "Dear, you *always* do that the same way every year." Saying these two words is like waving a red flag in front of a bull. They stop most conversations and start more quarrels than any other words in the dictionary.

Let's get specific. A close friend who is like an adopted mother to me had been thinking much about admiring her husband of forty years and decided Thanksgiving would be the perfect time to express her feelings. Approaching him that morning, she told him that on this Thanksgiving she was thankful for him, for his protective care of her all the years of their marriage, for his abundant provision, and for the security and satisfaction he had given her. She told him she was probably the most secure and protected woman in the world. She said her husband strutted around like a peacock the rest of the day. Previously she had admired her husband for his tenderness, thoughtfulness, and kindness, and he had never been so visibly pleased.

Tenderness, thoughtfulness, and kindness are godly and important qualities, but a man *also* needs to know that he is a man to you, that he is providing, protecting, and caring for you. As one woman put it, "Admire his masculinity!"

Keep these additional characteristics in mind as you

seek to admire your husband: leadership ability, mental capacity, superior strength, sexual capacity, steadfastness, courage, logical mind, financial expertise, and athletic skill.

Your superstar. Take out a sheet of paper, and write down every quality you can admire about your husband. List physical qualities, then emotional, intellectual, and spiritual ones. Now that you know your husband's admirable qualities, why keep them to yourself? It's good to admire your husband secretly, but how much better to admire him actively! Reverence is putting your total partner acceptance into practice. So start practicing! No excuses. You've made your list and have lots of admirable qualities to choose from. Now it's simply a matter of opening your mouth and saying what you know to be true. You may feel awkward at first, but do it anyway.

Advice from a man. I asked a good friend, who has a *creative counterpart* for a wife, to list examples of the way his wife verbally shows her admiration for him and to express the way it makes him feel. He wrote the following:

> Joanne doesn't just tell me that I have a nice build, she says, "I love your wonderful body. I like to run my hands over the muscles in your back."
>
> Once when jogging together she said, "I was watching you run ahead of me. Your form is so effortless and graceful. No wonder I can't keep up with you." (The next day I knocked 1:5 minutes off my best time!)
>
> Late one evening, after a hard day, she said, "Thank you for working so hard to give us this home and all the material things we have. Sometimes I feel

we just aren't appreciative enough of all you do." I could hardly wait to get to the office the next day!

Not long ago we went over insurance, wills, and our financial situation. Joanne said, "I just can't believe how well you take care of me. You handle the present problems, which are plenty; but you even have our future planned."

It's hard to express how her admiration makes me feel, to put it on paper, but it makes me want to be more of a man to her. It challenges me to grow (Lord knows I need it), to be stronger in my spiritual life. Maybe it's her striving to perfect our relationship that challenges me. She communicates by her admiration that she is truly interested in me as a person and in what I do. She makes me feel like a king.

What do you communicate to your husband? One wise woman put it like this: "I told *God* about his bad points, and I told *him* about his good points."

7

The Executive Vice President

A man walked into a library and asked the librarian for a copy of the book *Man the Master of Woman*. Without looking up, she pointed and said, "Sir, the fiction is in that corner."

Beginning in 1963 with the publication of *The Feminine Mystique*, there has been a re-examination of the numerous passages in the Bible regarding woman, her femininity, and the woman's role in the home. Particular scorn has been heaped upon the word *submission*. What is the woman's role? And more important, what does the Bible say about it?

There are three basic plans for marital happiness under consideration in our world today.

THREE MARITAL PLANS

PLAN A—THE PRESIDENT

Plan A says the decisions in the family should be made by the one who is most qualified. Plan A results in competition between husband and wife, and here is how it operates.[1]

The husband. He begins by *reasoning from confusion.* He has heard the rumor that he is supposed to be the head of the home. However, after observing his wife's behavior, he sees he is not getting any votes. Thus he begins to reason he is not the most qualified to make decisions (and in many areas he may not be). He can't act in confidence because he is not sure he will be supported by his wife. As a result, he retreats from leadership. Since every decision-making process ends in a battle and since he sees his wife is actually more qualified in some areas, he turns the reins over to her.

Gradually, however, he begins to *resent* his wife. He fumes internally over the fact that she will not respect his basic desire to lead the family. This ultimately comes to open *reaction*. Whenever she makes a mistake, he brings it to her attention. He now wants to prove she is wrong, and competition sets in. The end result of such a marriage is that all too frequently he runs elsewhere for total expression and fulfillment. He wants someone to respect him. He may find it in sports, his male friends, his children, his business or, of course, another woman. This is often not out of a desire for sexual variety but out of an emotional need to be admired and respected.

The wife. She generally begins by *reasoning from pride*. She asks, "Who is most qualified?" And she answers, "I am." She sees her husband as someone who is very human and who makes mistakes, and she wants to take over. As a result she *rejects* his leadership. She no longer encourages him to be the head of the home. Then paradoxically, when her husband seems uninterested in family involvement, she begins to *resent* him for not taking leadership. When she makes a wrong decision, she blames him. This leads to a stronger *reaction* against his lack of leadership. She frequently runs elsewhere, too. She buries her life in the children, a job, women's Bible studies, social activities, or another man. Key word: *compete*.

PLAN B—THE HOUSEKEEPER

Plan B says the husband is the head or leader, but the wife is not really a helpmate. She is not committed to being a *creative counterpart*. She is the woman who thinks marriage begins when she sinks into his arms and ends with her arms in the sink. When the survey takers arrive at her door with the question, "And, Mrs. Smith, what is your occupation?" she sadly replies, "Oh, I'm just a housewife." As one woman aptly put it, "I'm a wife to a man, not a house!"

A woman caught in the housekeeper syndrome usually has some or all of the following characteristics: very dependent, little emotional control, very subjective, indecisive, and very passive. She is uninterested in growing as a person and feels her plight in life is to submit to her husband, raise his children, and keep his house clean. She becomes boring as a person and lives in a dull routine. Often the television set becomes her constant companion to help her escape from boredom. Because she is unfulfilled she begins to *complain* and fits well into Solomon's description, *"The contentions of a wife are a continual dripping"* (Prov. 19:13). She is the one who caused Solomon to say it is better to live in the corner of an attic than in a beautiful home with a contentious woman (see Prov. 21:9).

The word that describes her is *complain*, and because she complains her husband usually complains, too—about her. And the couples in Plan B are caught in a vicious cycle that produces heartache and bitterness. Key word: *complain*.

PLAN C—THE CREATIVE COUNTERPART

God's plan for marital happiness involves a *spiritual head* and a *creative counterpart.* Instead of competing with each other as in Plan A and complaining to each other as in Plan B, God's man and God's woman *complete* each other.

A *creative counterpart* is a helpmate, a complement to her husband. She not only allows her husband to be the leader but also encourages him to take the leadership by reverencing him and by being submissive to him. She has chosen to be submissive because God has commanded it and because she is convinced that only *completion* will result in a vital, fulfilling marriage.

She is submissive, but strives to be capable, intelligent, industrious, organized, efficient, warm, tender, gracious—all virtues we saw in the beautiful blueprint in Proverb 31. She is not the president as in Plan A or the housekeeper in Plan B but the executive vice-president. Key word: *complete.*

THE MEANING OF HELPMATE

SLAVE OR COUNTERPART?

The role of helpmate indicates not a status of inferiority but a functional difference. The wife is in submission to her husband in the same way Christ is in submission to the Father. Yet Christ and the Father are equal and one! There cannot be two leaders. The purpose is functional teamwork that allows two people to complement each other, not compete with each other, in life.

Women sometimes say, "Don't say submission so loudly!" I hope to show you that submission is not a dirty word, but your hope of becoming all that God intended—and all that you desire!

Christ is subject to God. He is equal to God, He is very God, but He is subject to the Father. Jesus, Creator of heaven and earth, submitted Himself to God and took His place in the chain of authority. It is no shame or dishonor for a wife to be under authority if the Lord Jesus was. Each marriage partner has a blessed, unique responsibility, a purpose in life that the other cannot possibly fulfill and cannot happily exist without.

Henry Brandt expressed it this way in a speech I heard:

> The husband and wife are similar to the President and Vice President (let's make that Executive Vice President) of a bank. Both carry heavy responsibilities, help make policies, and live in accord with and are limited by the policies. On occasion, when a meeting of minds is impossible, the President must make the final decision. The husband is the head of the wife but the relationship should involve loyalty, good will, confidence and deep understanding.

I remember several years ago listening to a discussion around the dinner table. Joy, Robin, and Tommy entered into a "serious discussion" about who was the "boss" of the family. They talked back and forth, and finally five-year-old Robin said, "I know. Daddy's the big boss and Mommy's the little boss!" The other two nodded approvingly. A pretty good explanation for a five year old!

YOUR ATTITUDE IS SHOWING

Submission is an attitude as well as an action. A wife may feel that when she exhibits an act or two that seems to indicate submission she has done her bit.

One writer says that submissiveness is a matter not of mere outward form but of inner attitude. A wife can be a person of strong opinions and still be submissive to her husband's authority if deep down she respects him and is quite prepared and content for him to make and carry out the final decision. On the other hand, a wife who scarcely opens her mouth with an idea of her own and never questions her husband's decisions may, underneath it all, nurse a deep, sullen rebellion.[2]

THE DIVINE IDEAL

The divine ideal for maximum marriage is summed up in Ephesians 5:21–28. It is a beautiful picture and involves a husband and a wife completing each other through assigned role relationships.

MUTUAL SUBMISSION

> Submitting to one another in the fear of God. Wives, submit to your own husbands, as to the Lord. For the husband is the head of the wife, as also Christ is head of the church; and He is the Savior of the body. Therefore, just as the church is subject to Christ, so let the wives be to their own husbands in everything (Eph. 5:21–24).

Note that the passage opens with the words, "Submitting to one another in the fear of God." This verse says that *everyone* is to submit, not just wives. (Good news!) What does it mean?

Professor Howard Hendricks answers like this:

> As members of the body of Christ, we all need each
> other. We are committed to each other because we
> are the family of God. By the control of the Holy
> Spirit, we are to subject ourselves to each other to
> willingly yield to the needs, decisions, and ideas
> of those with whom we are in daily contact. The
> *natural* thing is to demand our rights and to not
> submit to anyone; it is the *supernatural* thing to be
> unselfish and to submit to one another.[3]

A wife is to submit to her husband in everything. I
asked my husband what total submission meant to him,
and he said he could summarize it in two words—*no
resistance*. (Ouch!) He went on to explain that submission also carries with it the responsibility of a wife to
tell her husband *exactly* how she feels on every issue
of their life together, so there will be no misunderstand-
ing. With an attitude of love, she should share her view
with her husband. Her general approach should be
something like this: "Honey, this is my viewpoint, and
I ask you to consider it. The final decision, however,
rests with you, and I will joyfully [that word is the
killer] go along with whatever you decide." Sometimes
a wife will appear to go along with her husband's decisions, but she will sulk or pout in silence. My husband
says that's worse than words.

Our marriage is a partnership, but Jody is the head
partner. Usually we agree on decisions, ideas, and goals,
but no two partners always agree on everything. When
I disagree with him, I lovingly present my reasons, then
leave the final decision with him. This is *no resistance*.
God knows what He is doing. If it turns out that I was

correct and Jody's decision was wrong, God will let him know.

In our home, Jody is the disciplinarian. I almost always agree with the way he handles the children. We discuss it, read books together, and share all our ideas. Deep down though, I'm an old softy, and the children know it. "Good old Mom will always understand." There have been times when I have disagreed with the way the children should be disciplined and I was overruled. At times it has been extremely difficult to go along *joyfully* with Jody's decision, without arguing in front of the children. Later, when I began to see the good effect of strong discipline, I was glad Jody had decided as he did.

Years ago Jody and I had a financial decision to make concerning our marriage organization. We discussed our ideas and found we had totally opposite views. The more we talked, the more we disagreed!

Therefore, Jody decided to counsel with five mature Christian laymen, and all five agreed with him. Six men on one side and me on the other! After much prayer and consideration, Jody decided with the majority.

Never have I struggled so much with being *joyful*. In my will I accepted the decision, but in my emotions I was screaming, "I'm right." I prayed often about my attitude and felt it was changing—that is, until I had my dream.

A week after Jody made this financial decision I dreamed he was put on trial and all the jurors proved him wrong and me right! I'd won! I awoke feeling sick to my stomach and said, "Oh, God, I've tried in every way I know to give this to You and then I dream this

dream. I again give it to You, Lord, I do want to have
the right response." My attitude gradually did change
as I continued to claim God's promises.

I remember another situation in 1977 when I was
writing the first edition of Creative Counterpart and
Jody was writing Solomon on Sex. He had written four
pages on the sexual relationship that I felt were too
specific and too blunt. I felt the Christian world was
not ready for these four pages and told Jody if they
were printed, I'd have to hide in the house for months
because I was sure people would point at me and say,
"I bet she even does those things." Jody responded
that the four pages were great and that the Christian
public definitely needed to read them! Obviously we
were at an impasse. Because Jody lovingly accuses me
of "emoting" off the top of my head, I decided to write
out my reasons very logically and present them to him.
I prayed about the situation and told the Lord I would
declare loudly in love my viewpoint and then trust
Him to show Jody what was right. Gulping down my
fears, I handed Jody my list and told him I wanted
him to consider once more what I thought. I assured
him, "I will leave the decision to you and trust God
to show you what to do with those four pages." After
reading my "logic," he smiled at me and without a
word took a red pen and crossed out all four pages! I
was, of course, jubilant. I could be seen on the streets
without fear.

In some other situations in our marriage Jody has
changed his view when I've shared my ideas with him.
The issue, however, is not who wins but how we respond.

The passage on submission sounds as if our husbands

got together and wrote it, doesn't it? They didn't; God did! Please note that God does not say your husband has earned the right to be your head or has deserved it. He says that He, God, decided this was the best plan and therefore asks you to honor the plan. God had many plans available to Him, and He chose this one. Believe it or not, it's to your advantage!

So far this seems like a one-way street: the wife is to submit. But hold on. The husband has an even greater responsibility: to love his wife *as Christ loved the church.*

A HUSBAND'S ALL-OUT LOVE

In the biblical view of marriage the submission of the wife is always set in the context of the total love of the husband.

> Husbands, love your wives, just as Christ also loved the church and gave Himself for it. . . . So husbands ought to love their own wives as their own bodies; he who loves his wife loves himself. For no one ever hated his own flesh, but nourishes and cherishes it, just as the Lord does the church (Eph. 5:25, 28–29).

The husband is to love his wife as Christ loved the church. (That's it, Paul! Preach it!) No one could ever measure a love that great. I'm ready for it. How about you? I can hear many of you saying, "This commandment wouldn't be so bad *if* my husband would love me as Christ loved the church and *if* he loved me as his own body. Maybe then submission would be a natural thing."

I personally believe it would become more natural. No woman will have difficulty with submission if she is being loved like that. I am blessed to have a godly husband who seeks to obey God and love me totally! You're right in thinking I have it easier than many wives. But at the same time God requires more of me in my response to Jody. To whom much is given, the Bible says, much will be required (see Luke 12:48).

God never said submission was easy (and I agree), but He did say that of all the plans available to Him, the model of husband as *spiritual head* and wife as *helpmate* was the most perfect for the physical, emotional, and spiritual welfare of both partners.

Let's look at some of the barriers to a submissive spirit, as well as some of the benefits and limits of submission.

THE BARRIERS TO A SUBMISSIVE SPIRIT

BARRIER 1—THE DISOBEDIENT HUSBAND

First let me say that I rarely meet an obedient wife! As I pointed out, any wife who faithfully applies the "three A's" (*acceptance, admiration,* submission to his *authority*) will almost inevitably see her husband begin to change. The problem is that a wife wants push-button results, the American way, after applying a few principles for a week or so. I must emphasize that a wife is to apply these principles so that she can follow in His steps and *not* so that she can effect a change in her husband. She does these things because it is part of being a Christian and not because it is a way to get her husband to change.

If a wife's motivation is to effect a change in her

husband and if after applying the "three A's" for a brief time she sees no change, obviously her motivation to continue will fade. As one woman said to me, "Oh, I've tried all of that, and it didn't work." Actually she had tried it for a week or so and only halfheartedly at that. Furthermore, her efforts were all external; inwardly her spirit was full of resentment and bitterness.

BARRIER 2—AN ARBITRARY DISCRIMINATION BASED ON SEX

Why should the woman be the one to submit? Why can't it be mutual? First of all, let me say that in the biblical view of marriage, it is mutual. The wife is to fully express her views, disagree anytime she feels it, and the couple should mutually come to decisions agreed upon by both. This is always the case in a marriage that is truly Christian, because the word *submission* is set in the context of the husband loving the wife as Christ loved the church. A woman who is being loved by a man in such a way that he puts her interests, desires, and dreams above his own hardly has any trouble being submissive. That is the true biblical picture of marriage.

But second, I must admit that this arrangement is arbitrary discrimination based on sex. However, it is *not* unjustly arbitrary. Everything God does is for the best for His children. He set it up this way because in His infinite love and wisdom He knows this is the best arrangement. On what other terms should the *head* and *helpmate* be determined? On who is "most qualified"? If that were the basis, there would be nothing but debate on who is the most qualified on every point, and marriage would end up in perpetual competition instead of completion. God's way is totally unrelated to the basic qualifications of intrinsic merits of the husband and the wife. It is a purely functional setup, as in a corporate chain of command.

BARRIER 3—A SQUELCHING OF PERSONAL IDENTITY

Some critics of submission have argued that such a view of marriage "dehumanizes" women and results in a total loss of personal identity. To be submissive is to become submerged in "some man," and as a result, American homemakers are not able to find out who they really are. However, since biblical submission is set in the context of the husband loving his wife as Christ loved the church, it is hard for me to see how such a loss of identity could take place.

My husband wants me to be the most fulfilled woman alive! He would do almost anything to help me find my identity. But beyond that, a woman in a potential situation of submerged identity may be that way not because she has submitted to her husband but because she has not made any attempts to reach out, develop outside interests, meet people, and develop her mind. Instead she has stayed around the house all day watching soap operas and superintending (or screaming at) small children.

Paradoxically, Jesus said one does not find personal identity by demanding rights and rejecting the biblical view of marriage. On the contrary, "For whoever desires to save his life will lose it, but whoever loses his life for My sake and the gospel's will save it" (Mark 8:35). We find our identity not by focusing on "who we are" but by denying ourselves. Out of death comes real life!

A woman finds her identity by denying herself for her husband and her children and other people. A man finds his identity by denying himself and living for his wife and children. It is in self-denial that true inward qualities are wrought and a beautiful life is developed.

BARRIER 4—THE FOUR FEARS

There are four basic reasons why a wife is afraid to submit to the authority of her husband.

1. *She is afraid of what he might do or ask her to do.* The first thing some women say when hearing about submission is, "But he'll ask me to mate swap." It's true that a husband might ask his wife to do something wrong, and I hope to answer some questions about this later in the chapter (see "The Limits of Submission"). In most cases, however, a wife is really afraid that her husband might ask her to do several things that she just doesn't want to do!

2. *She is afraid he will fail.* It's possible, of course, that God wants her husband to fail occasionally, since everyone grows through trials and failure. One of the hardest things I've ever had to do was step out of the way and let my husband fail. I try hard to say, "God, he's Yours. I love him and don't want him to ever be hurt, but Lord, don't let me get in Your way. If this trying situation is for his growth, let me love him and encourage him and stand behind him, but keep me out of Your way." I have to fight my tendency to be the "mother" and to step in and take over when the going gets rough!

3. *She is afraid of his irresponsibility.* A wife who simply yields everything to her husband when his past track record is one of never assuming responsibility

for what she yields up will naturally have some fears. What will happen to her? To the children? There may be situations in which she should gradually turn things over to him. To dump everything on him all at once could overwhelm him. But frequently a man fails to assume responsibility because he is not receiving a loving dose of the "three A's."

Once the responsibility is clearly his and he sees his wife is not going to fight him about every point on a particular issue anymore, more often than not, he will begin to feel the weight of that responsibility and assume it. Then, as he assumes it, if he finds that his wife consistently admires him when he takes a step and unconditionally accepts him when he makes a mistake, he will be motivated to develop his potential!

4. *She is afraid of God's will.* A wife may agree with everything that has been discussed about these three fears, but when it comes to applying it in real life, another fear surfaces. It is the fear that God may allow the situation to go on for too long or that He might allow too intense a hurt to occur. In effect it is a fear of God's will and a lack of trust in Him. It is almost as if she thinks God is unconcerned about her, as if she thinks He really doesn't love her. After all, He would never cause her to make such choices if He really loved her, would He?

God has clearly demonstrated His love in sending His only Son to die for us, so there is no question of His love. If the hurt were to continue for a long time and if it were to be intense, no one would be more grieved than our heavenly Father. Yet if He allows it, it is clearly for the individual's ultimate good (see Rom. 8:28). From God's viewpoint, the trials someone goes through are not nearly as important as the responses she makes to them.

Sharon was a beautiful, intelligent woman and a new Christian when her husband left her and moved to another state to enjoy wine, women, and song. Many people called her a fool during the years she waited and loved him and strived to be submissive in spite of her circumstances. She shared this beautiful quote from Alan Redpath, which she memorized and claimed during that difficult time:

> There is nothing—no circumstance, no trouble, *no testing*—that can ever touch me until, first of all, it has gone past God and past Christ right through to me. If it has come that far, it has come with a *great purpose*, which I may not understand at the moment. But as I *refuse* to become panicky, as I lift up my eyes to Him and accept it as coming from the throne of God for some *great purpose* of *blessing* to my own heart, no sorrow will ever disturb me, no trial will *ever* disarm me, *no circumstance will cause me to fret*—for *I shall rest in the joy of what my Lord is!*—That is the rest of victory![4]

Many who rose in horror and wailed "fool" became silent when her husband returned and deeply committed himself to her and the children.

These four fears comprise the biggest single barrier to submission. They are real and may cause a sincere wife great emotional distress. However, these fears must be set against the background of a loving heavenly Father who is the blessed Controller of all things. God is alive and well today! He is not just an abstract theory but a living Person who actually invades lives, changes situations, protects His children, and gives comfort.

Instead of letting fears repeat over and over in her head like a broken record, a woman should put those fears in God's hands. Then she needs to have the faith and courage to stand and wait for Him to deal with them.

The pattern is quite biblical. Look at Sarah, Abraham's wife. Sarah obeyed Abraham and called him her master. But then an Old Testament saint like Abraham was probably the perfect husband, right? Not on your life!

Once while traveling in Egypt, Abraham feared for his life when he heard that the Pharaoh had his eye on Sarah. So to save his own skin, he told the Pharaoh that Sarah was his sister, not his wife. The Pharaoh then proceeded to take Sarah into his harem! Did Sarah scream "rape"? Did she cry, kick, or throw a tantrum? No. Trusting God, she submitted to Abraham's pathetic plan and went into the Pharaoh's harem.

Most of us would never sit still for such a thing, but Sarah knew God would work it out, somehow. So she waited. God told the Pharaoh that Sarah was Abraham's wife and warned him of impending wrath. The Pharaoh was so terrified of Abraham's God that he took Sarah to Abraham and asked them to leave the country immediately. Sarah gave God time to work in the situation—and He did! She placed her trust in God and did not give way to fear.

If the Pharaoh had come to Sarah to have sexual relations, she would have been forced to tell him the truth, but God never allowed that situation to happen. He intervened and solved the problem Himself. Most of us are so quick to open our mouths that we never give God a chance to work.

Peter says we are Sarah's daughters if we do what

is right and do not give way to fear (see 1 Pet. 3:5–6). The whole Bible testifies to this. Let's start taking our Christianity seriously. It is a supernatural faith!

BARRIER 5—PRIDE

This barrier is perhaps the most common of all. When a husband and a wife disagree, the wife may think that she can do a better job or that she has superior insights. For example, let's say the husband wants to discipline the children in a certain way. A wife often retorts, "What do you know about it? I'm home with the children all day, and I know what they need better than you do!"

A man faces this daily with his employer. When he and his boss disagree about how things should be done, it often becomes a problem of pride. Far better for both the wife and the employee to forcefully and freely express their views and leave the decision up to the husband or the employer rather than make a continual contest out of it. If a husband makes a wrong decision and against the counsel of his wife, that becomes a matter between him and God, and he doesn't need an I-told-you-so spirit emanating from his *creative counterpart!*

THE BENEFITS OF A SUBMISSIVE SPIRIT

The first benefit is that you glorify God by being obedient to His commandment. That is exciting, and there are practical benefits for us right where we live, too!

TENSION RELEASER

I believe submission is one solution to tension, tiredness, and pressure. Too often a woman's tension, tiredness, and headaches are a result of absorbing responsibilities God never intended her to have.

Mary and Chuck were a couple locked in the cycle of competition. She felt responsible for every decision, from the family business they ran together to the clothes he wore! She pressed, connived, and pressured to get her way. The right decision was *her* decision.

The stress and tension Mary experienced showed on her face. She hated the word *submission* and fought against any plan that said she was not the leader.

After attending the Creative Counterpart Seminar, Mary did an about-face. She saw God and the beauty of His plan and made a commitment to be submissive to her husband. She actually made her commitment in the form of a contract with God, and here it is:

> I, today, Wednesday, November 20, vow to myself, not to suggest, tell, nag, or criticize my husband on how to run his business. I will bite my tongue, leave the premises or do whatever is necessary, so as not to force my opinion. My knowing that my opinions are right will be satisfaction enough—no one else need share how sweet and terrific I really am! I am now willing to accept his business failure to enforce this rule! I will read this each day before I start work. If I should fail to achieve this goal even twice, I will quit my job knowing it is a hindrance to my becoming a *creative counterpart.*

Mary recently told me that "life has changed from 'totally serious' to 'fun and enjoyable.' I never realized the pressure and tension I was under."

HUSBAND CHANGER

Submission is your only hope of changing your husband. Your husband will change as you allow him to be head of his home and as you are submissive to him. He will not change by your nagging, belittling, suggesting, reminding, or mothering.

Jody and I were married as college students. I had worked while in college, had a scholarship, and knew that money was hard to come by. Jody had not worked and did not know that money was hard to come by. Guess who was more responsible with the finances? Guess who let it be known that she was the more responsible? Innumerable arguments resulted from my desire to know how every penny was spent. Jody, a book addict, finally began to smuggle books he had purchased into the house and put them on the shelf where I wouldn't see them. Then when I would notice a book and ask him if it were new, he would smile and say, "Oh, no, Honey. I've had it for months!"

Later, when I began to understand what God wanted me to be as a wife, I totally let go of the finances. I did it with fear and trembling, but I did it! I was submissive to Jody and began to pray that God would make him faithful in this area.

Today, Jody is so faithful with our finances, I sometimes wonder if I prayed the right prayer. We are free from debt, pay cash for our purchases, and have a detailed budget. We have several credit cards but rarely use them. I greatly respect Jody for his policy, "Don't buy it until you have the money." The tables have been turned, and now I come to him to ask forgiveness for charging something that was on sale. Jody speaks often at seminars on the subject of finances and teaches other men about how to be financially faithful. This was the man I didn't trust with a dime!

One woman who became a Christian after several years of marriage realized that her marriage was a case of total role reversal—she was the leader and her husband the helper. She was aggressive and outgoing, and he was not. After struggling to discern what God wanted to do in her marriage, she decided to be submissive to her husband, even though she feared he wouldn't lead. Later, she wrote me:

> I really believe a Christian man can't be the man God intended until his wife is submissive and fits in with his plans. As I'm learning to do this, Mike is getting more confidence. We really share and talk more. In intimate matters, things are much improved. I realized that I hadn't been meeting his needs in any way. I'm convinced that if wives will go to the Lord, ask Him to make us submissive, and then obey (that's what hurts), then the Lord will really make our homes the picture of Christ and the church!

YOUR SEXUAL RESPONSE

Submission is many times a key to sexual response. According to a survey we personally conducted among two thousand Christian women, 39 percent of those who had been married twenty years indicated they have experienced an orgasm sometimes, rarely, or never. This is one of the most common problems women bring to marriage counselors. The reason is that sexual response at the physical level is the equivalent of submission at the psychological level. Men and women view sexual intercourse from different perspectives. A man tends to see it as a "taking" or a "possessing." A woman, on the other hand, tends to conceptualize it as a "yielding up" of herself. Obviously, if a woman does see sexual intercourse as a yielding up and if she is in continual rebellion against and disobedience to her husband, these feelings can carry over to the marriage bed and can block her ability to respond.

THE LIMITS OF SUBMISSION

In Acts 5:1–11 we read the story of Ananias and Sapphira. This couple sold a piece of land and agreed together to keep some of the proceeds and lie about the amount they gleaned from the sale. The husband went alone to take the money to the disciples, lied to them, and immediately fell dead. Three hours later, his wife appeared on the scene and, as prearranged, repeated the same lie. The apostle Peter said to her, "How is it that you have agreed together to test the Spirit of the Lord?" And she, too, fell dead.

Some have said that a wife who is totally submissive to her husband is not responsible to God if her husband causes her to sin. This passage proves otherwise. Each human being is responsible for his or her own sins. The limit of submission is this: total submission without personal sin.

WHEN CAN A WIFE DISOBEY?

1. *When a husband asks his wife to do something directly contrary to Scripture.* An individual's conscience is not always a reliable guide, and neither is the feeling of being led by the Lord. The Book is the guide to trust.

2. *When she has worked through the following program:*[5]

- She should ask, "What is the need in my husband's life behind the request he is making?"
- She should suggest a creative way of meeting

that basic need without resorting to contradicting Scripture.

- She should trust God as Sarah did. God may
  want to intervene and demonstrate His power.

Suppose, for instance, a husband asks his wife to
get an abortion. She needs to first ask, "Is having an
abortion contrary to Scripture?" The answer is yes.

Second, she needs to ask, "What is the need in my
husband's life behind asking me to have an abortion?"
Perhaps the couple has several children already, and
the husband is afraid of having another to provide for.
Perhaps the wife is no longer a wife, but only a mother,
and the husband views the child as another threat. Perhaps he's afraid of losing his job and feels it's no time
to have a child. There could be many reasons.

After discerning the basic need, the wife should suggest a creative way of meeting that basic need without
resorting to contradicting Scripture. Perhaps she could
admit her failure as a wife, ask forgiveness, and show
him what a fantastic wife she can be! If money were
the issue, perhaps she could offer to bring in additional
income. She can be creative if she gets her mind out
of its rut and tries!

I offer these limits of submission because I realize
that bizarre situations can occur. The Hebrew midwives
broke the absolute of not telling a lie in order to protect
the newborn from Pharaoh's hands (see Ex. 1:15–22).
Even the Lord Jesus was willing to break the law of
the Sabbath in order to meet the need of human hunger
(see Mark 2:23). Furthermore, He justified David's viola-
tion of the Biblical absolute against non-priests eating
from the table of the showbread, recognizing David's
need at that time for food (see Mark 2:25).

Today wife-abuse is a common occurrence and, sadly, is seen sometimes in Christian marriages. Submission does not mean allowing another person to batter us, whether the battering is physical, verbal, or emotional.

A REAL ORNAMENT

We read in 1 Peter 3 that a woman should have the "incorruptible ornament of a gentle and quiet spirit, which is very precious in the sight of God" (v. 4). The Greek word for *precious* is used two other times in 1 Peter. First, the shed blood of Jesus Christ is precious (see 1:19), and second, He is the precious cornerstone of our faith (see 2:6). The third time it is in reference to a godly, submissive woman. God says we, too, can be precious as the Lord Jesus is. A calm, gentle, submissive spirit is rare and costly and of great worth to God. If you have ever met a woman such as this, you have not forgotten her. She is precious to God, a glory to her husband, and a joy to be around!

❧ 8 ❧

Inherit a Blessing

One day Jody came home from a long and exhausting trip. The next morning when he got ready to mow the lawn, he noticed that the next-door neighbor had dug a trench on the property line between our lawn and his. This neighbor was apparently concerned that water on our lawn might somehow trickle into his territory.

How would you respond if you were confronted with a situation like this? The implied insult in this trench-digging exercise could motivate one to retaliate in some way. Many neighborhood conflicts have their roots in trivial little insults made by one neighbor, which result in returned insults from the other neighbor. An insult-for-insult relationship develops, and all avenues for friendship and communication disappear. Not only are many neighborhood conflicts characterized by this insult-for-insult relationship, but many marriages, unfortunately, fall into the same trap.

In the chapter on unconditional acceptance, I suggested an exercise in which you divide a sheet of paper into two columns and then note your mate's weaknesses in the left-hand column and your wrong responses in the right-hand column. In a counseling session with one woman, the following exchange took place:

COUNSELOR: What are your husband's strengths?

WOMAN: He doesn't have any.

COUNSELOR: You must have had something that drew you to him when you married.

WOMAN: That's why I'm here! I can't figure out why I married him!

The counselor continued to press in order to determine the list of the husband's strengths. After several minutes of probing, he finally discovered something when he asked, "Does he give you any money?"

The woman mentioned an extremely large sum of money. Excitedly, the counselor said, "All right, there's a strength—money!" However, he was looking for more than just one item, so he continued the search. He asked her if she owned a car.

WOMAN: Bob gave me a new Eldorado for my birthday two months ago.

COUNSELOR: An Eldorado—that's a strength!

He didn't have much, but at least there was a start. However, there was a noticeable turnaround in her attitude when the counselor began to ask her about Bob's weaknesses; she lighted up. That's what she had come to discuss. The first weakness she mentioned was food.

WOMAN: All he does is eat, eat, eat. He's 272 pounds and growing.

Then she brought up a second weakness.

WOMAN: He doesn't pay any attention to me. When he comes home in the evening, he walks right to the phone. He doesn't even acknowledge that I exist.

She elaborated on this for some time, and then she added a third weakness.

WOMAN: My husband is a Christian, but sometimes he gets so mad that he swears at me.

The woman continued to enumerate other weaknesses. It was simply amazing to observe the ease with which these weaknesses flowed out of her mouth in contrast to her total blank when it came to describing her husband's strengths. The counselor finally moved to the right-hand column, her wrong responses.

COUNSELOR: What do you do when your husband does these things?

The woman appeared perplexed and said, "What do you mean?" She apparently had no capacity to understand that she was doing anything wrong in response to his weaknesses. The counselor persisted and asked the question in a different way.

COUNSELOR: When your husband does these things that irritate you, how do you respond?

She gave an illustration of a typical response. At an executive party where Bob wanted to impress his boss, she saw that her overweight husband was at the refreshment table across the den. She yelled so everyone could hear her, "Roll on over here, Bob."

The counselor made a note and then asked another question.

COUNSELOR: What do you do when he doesn't pay attention to you?

WOMAN: I don't pay attention to him.

COUNSELOR: And if he swears at you?

WOMAN: I swear at him.

This woman's whole approach to her marriage was to give insult for insult. When she'd been wounded or offended or hurt, her initial response, a very human one, was to return the insult.

In this chapter I want to address the issue of the kind of response we should make when our husbands offend us or in some other way wound our feelings. I believe this deals with one of the most vital and fundamental concepts of the New Testament: responding with a blessing.

In 1 Peter 3:8–12 the apostle gives us specific information regarding what we should do when we have been wounded or offended by our husbands and how we should do it. Let's take a look at this exciting concept together.

WHAT WE SHOULD DO

The first seven verses of 1 Peter 3 deal with husband-wife relationships. Peter speaks primarily of the wife's submission and trust and of the husband's responsibility to be understanding and respectful. Then in verses 8 and 9 he summarizes a key principle for bringing about harmonious husband-wife relationships:

> Finally, all of you live in harmony with one another; be sympathetic, love as brothers, be compassionate and humble. Do not repay evil with evil or insult with insult, but with blessing, because to this you were called so that you may inherit a blessing (NIV).

Two kinds of relationships are described: (1) the insult-for-insult relationship and (2) the blessing-for-insult relationship. We all have an idea of what it means to be insulted or offended by our mates. The focus here, however, is not on the insult but on the response to it. God asks us to respond to an insult with a blessing. This is contrary to all of our natural feelings. When we are hurt, we want to hurt back. When we are insulted, we want to return the insult. Our natural response is to take a step forward and hit back, but God asks us to take a step back, breathe in deeply, and return a blessing.

Can you imagine responding like this if you've been wounded or hurt? Without question this is one of the most humbling, difficult-to-obey exhortations found in all the Scriptures and yet the benefits can be dramatic.

I remember once listening to a message by Dr. Henry Brandt, a Christian psychologist. He described a way in which his wife had responded with a blessing by quiet prayer at a time when he had been rude and offensive. Apparently they were on their way to teach at a marriage seminar for several hundred people in Chicago. It wasn't every trip that his wife was able to join him, so they decided to really splurge and make this one a kind of second honeymoon. They spent a wonderful night together in a luxurious hotel, which was located just off the freeway halfway between Detroit and Chicago. As they pulled onto the freeway, his wife alerted him to the fact that he had accidentally turned the wrong way; instead of heading toward Chicago, they were actually headed toward Detroit. Dr. Brandt said he rudely dismissed her counsel with some deprecating remark about back-seat drivers and headed off in the direction of Detroit. Often when a husband reacts in this way, he is justified! A wife may be excellent at calling to her husband's attention, while driving, the fastest way to a certain destination; the proper speed at which to drive; his proximity to the car in front; his forgetfulness at making a turn; or many other irritating little helpful hints. My husband has often told me that he just can't understand how he is able to drive around Vienna, Austria, when I'm not in the car to give him all this guidance. Dr. Brandt's wife, however, had been wounded by his cutting remark, and she contemplated a response. Reflecting on the upcoming marriage seminar and the purpose of the time to get alone together, she wisely refrained from the impulse to insult and prayed silently that God would show her husband the proper direction to Chicago.

Dr. Brandt went on to say that fifteen minutes later, they saw a giant freeway sign with "Detroit 75 miles" on it. Mrs. Brandt remained silent, but Dr. Brandt felt the vibrations emanating from the right side of the front seat. There was no way he was going to acknowledge that he was wrong, so he felt he would press on until he found another sign. Fifteen minutes later, a big sign proclaimed: "Detroit 60 miles." By this time the vibrations emanating from the right-hand side of the front seat were becoming exceptionally strong, and as a result Dr. Brandt dug his heels in even further and decided to seek, believe it or not, one more sign. Thirty minutes later a freeway sign said, "Detroit 35 miles." By this time Dr. Brandt was fuming. He said he drove on aimlessly for another twenty minutes trying to figure out how to get to Chicago without turning around!

I remember in the early years of our marriage when I was first struggling with the principle of not giving insult for insult, Jody and I had an experience that we can now look back on rather humorously. In preparation for a series of messages on communication in marriage, Jody and I had been studying the passage in 1 Peter about returning a blessing for an insult.

That night Jody and I had an argument. I don't even remember what it was about, but he tells me his only recollection is that it was his fault. I'm the kind of person who needs immediate reconciliation. When there's any tension in the air, I often insist on "talking it through" immediately, thoroughly, and completely. However, many men are not like this, and Jody is one of them. He typically needs some time to let his emotions settle and the temperature cool down before he can comfortably enter into a meaningful exchange.

However, in my self-righteousness (after all, doesn't the Bible say, "Do not let the sun go down on your wrath"? [Eph. 4:26]), I insisted that we talk about it and talk about it and talk about it and talk about it. My insistence only made the situation worse, and finally Jody did something that was utterly incomprehensible to me. He rolled over and went to sleep. Jody tells me that in counseling with many men, he has found that some of them have honed this skill to a fine art. Any time the temperature of a conversation gets too heated or any time there is a demand being placed upon them for emotional support or thorough communication, they can simply turn it off, roll over, and go to sleep.

I laid awake half the night, staring at the ceiling and thinking all kinds of thoughts about how selfish he was. I worked myself into a frenzy before I was finally able to get to sleep about 3:00 A.M. The next morning was Saturday, Jody's only morning to sleep in. However, at the time we had three young children, so I didn't get to sleep in. I awoke that morning feeling really frustrated because of the disagreement the night before. What I wanted to do was reject Jody, slam the door to let him know I was mad, and then tell him how utterly selfish and unloving he was. I was irritated because as I tried to act out my anger, the verse we had been studying about returning a blessing for an insult kept running through my mind. It's hard to continue with a plan to return an insult when God's command to return a blessing is blaring at you.

So I finally said, "Okay, Lord, how do I return a blessing?" I knew myself well enough to know that if my mouth opened, an insult would come out. I went into the kitchen, prepared Jody his favorite breakfast of a bacon-and-cheese omelet, toast, and orange juice, and took it into the room about 9:00 when he was just waking up. As soon as Jody saw what I had done and remembered our disagreement of the night before, he was overcome with guilt. He reached over, took my head in his hands, and said, "Honey, I really love you, and I'm really sorry for last night." Later Jody told me that when I arrived at his bedside with breakfast, my action prompted him to dwell on a passage in Romans:

> Beloved, do not avenge yourselves, but rather give place to wrath; for it is written, "Vengeance is Mine, I will repay," says the Lord.

> "Therefore if your enemy hungers, feed him;
> If he thirsts, give him a drink;
> For in so doing you will heap coals of fire on his head" (12:19–20).

He said that breakfast in bed had been like "coals of fire on his head" and had convicted him of his guilt and wrong response.

I realize that not every woman who reads these pages is married to someone who is devoted to the Lord and to her and who will readily make these kinds of responses when God brings them to his attention. Returning a blessing is more difficult in such cases. Nevertheless, the principle is valid.

Like so many things in Scripture, these kinds of responses are utterly contrary to the environment in which we were raised and are therefore extremely difficult to implement. For example, the world says, "Strive to acquire material possessions and you will get them"; yet the Scriptures teach, "Seek first the kingdom of God and His righteousness, and all these things shall be added to you" (Matt. 6:33). The world teaches, "You get things by striving to acquire them"; but the Scripture admonishes, "Give, and it will be given to you" (Luke 6:38). The world says, "Love your neighbors and hate those who are your enemies"; but the Word of God counsels, "Love your enemies, bless those who curse you, do good to those who hate you, pray for those who spitefully use you and persecute you" (Matt. 5:44). A major teaching of the world propagated through the media and the advertising of the materialistic West is "a full and satisfying life comes from material security and money"; but in direct contrast the Scripture teaches, "Blessed are those who hunger and thirst for righteousness, / For they shall be filled" (Matt. 5:6).

It is not surprising, therefore, that the Bible's view of how to respond to an ungrateful or insensitive husband would sound rather strange when compared with most people's responses today.

WHY SHOULD WE RENDER A BLESSING?

One of the things that continually amazes me about the Scriptures is how practical and true to life they are. Anyone who has lived with a difficult husband or who has suffered through pain in a disintegrating marriage can only gasp in dismay when initially confronted with such an overwhelming responsibility: respond with a blessing when insulted and wounded. The apostle Peter was obviously a pastor. He knew the implications of what he was asking, and he knew the need to provide reasons for making this seemingly irrational response. We all have fears that we'll be walked upon, that we'll never have the opportunity to communicate our true feelings, that we'll be taken advantage of and, perhaps, that we'll end up condoning the sins of the persons who have offended us. Because Peter realized we would have these fears, he goes on to give us four reasons why we should respond with a blessing.

IT IS PART OF OUR CALLING AS CHRISTIANS

Peter tells us that we are to respond with a blessing because we were called to this so that we may inherit a blessing (see 1 Pet. 3:9). The first reason we are to respond this way is quite simply because it is part of our calling as Christians. Furthermore he tells us that if we make this response, there is reward, an inheritance. In this passage he seems to be referring to blessings in this life.

It is so important for us to grasp this first reason. I remember teaching on this subject at a marriage seminar, and several months later a woman came to me and said, "I tried this, but it didn't work." I said, "What do you mean?" She said, "Well, you talked about responding with a blessing and I worked on this for some time, but my husband never changed."

I cannot promise you that if you respond with a blessing when you're hurt or wounded your husband will change. I cannot promise you a life of happiness and personal fulfillment, but I can promise you that you are living according to your purpose and calling as a Christian; you are obeying the will of God and there is peace in obedience. The first reason you are to respond this way is not so that you can secure a hoped-for change in your mate, but because it is God's desire that you make this kind of response.

Karen married Jim believing he was a vibrant Christian. She had known him two years, and he had led a Christian group on their college campus. They married, but within a few months it became obvious that he was a Dr. Jekyll and Mr. Hyde. The wonderful Jim she had known was one side; a mean, vindictive, immoral

Jim was the other side. Her pain was indescribable. For her safety and mental health, she moved into a separate apartment.

As we talked she said, "Linda, I want to try to live 1 Peter 2 and 3 before Jim. He has hurt and insulted me beyond description, but I believe God wants me to return a blessing for an insult."

Karen went to live and counsel in a home for unwed mothers and waited on God for two years. During this time she continued to try to reach out to Jim and return a blessing. When Jim filed for divorce, Karen was at peace because she had been obedient.

IT IS THE KEY TO A HAPPY LIFE

Having laid that fundamental foundation, the apostle Peter expands upon the blessings that will come to us in this life if we follow God's way of response.

> He who would love life
> And see good days,
> Let him refrain his tongue from evil,
> And his lips from speaking guile;
> Let him turn away from evil and do good;
> Let him seek peace and pursue it (1 Pet. 3:10–
> 11).

Responding with a blessing involves at least three things: the restraint of the tongue, a decision of the will to turn from evil and do good, and an inner attitude that says, "I will seek peace and pursue it."

The apostle promises that the one who gives blessing instead of insult will have days free from frustration and tension. Have you ever met a bitter person? Refusing to respond with a blessing often results in bitterness and an unforgiving spirit. I have met a woman with lines in her face, hardened by years of bitterness. For each offense her husband has committed, she has steadfastly refused to respond in God's way; instead, she has rendered insult for insult. She is often full of fear. She can't trust her husband. She tends to misread every situation, and she has become incapable of genuine love for him. Bitterness and resentment eat away at people's insides, causing problems ranging from ulcers to eventual death. Giving a blessing lifts that burden.

IT PUTS GOD ON OUR SIDE

The apostle goes on to say in 1 Peter 3:12, "For the eyes of the LORD are on the righteous, / And his ears are open to their prayers." When we respond with a blessing, God joins our team. It is our responsibility to make the kind of responses that will bring honor to Christ. And when we do, God commits Himself to us and promises to attend to our prayers.

But what about the responsibilities of our husbands? Why has Peter failed to mention them? This is probably intentional because it is more important to God that we learn how to respond to hurt in a godly way than it is that we be delivered from the ones hurting us. One of the fundamental principles of life expressed throughout the Scriptures is that our responses are the things God wants to deal with first.

IT PUTS GOD AGAINST THOSE WHO OFFEND US

At the end of verse 12 the apostle counsels, "But the face of the LORD is against those who do evil."

Perhaps our greatest fear in responding with a blessing is the fear of what will happen to us. If we are being wounded and offended by others and we do not take up an offense or if we do not counterattack and take revenge, how will the offending parties ever be changed? Who will deal with "those who do evil"? Peter answers that "God will."

But what about the apparent lack of evidence that God is doing anything? Sometimes it seems we respond with a blessing and we're simply taken advantage of. Again we must refocus our attention. Why are we responding with a blessing? Is it because we hope to effect a change in our husbands? If it is, then our motivations are improper.

We respond with a blessing because it is part of our calling as Christians, but furthermore we need to remember that sometimes God can allow an offense to continue for an extensive period of time because He has other purposes in mind. Often they involve character building in our own lives. We are told in Hebrews, "Now faith is the substance of things hoped for, the evidence of things not seen" (11:1). The psalmist exhorts us,

> Commit your way to the LORD,
> Trust also in Him,
> And He shall bring it to pass.
> He shall bring forth your righteousness as the light,
> And your justice as the noonday.
> Rest in the LORD, and wait patiently for Him;
> Do not fret because of him who prospers in his
>   way,
> Because of the man who brings wicked schemes
>   to pass.
> Cease from anger, and forsake wrath;

Do not fret—it only causes harm.
For evildoers shall be cut off;
But those who wait on the LORD,
They shall inherit the earth (Ps. 37:5-9).

God promises that He will deal with those who offend us. When we respond with an insult or seek revenge, we are assuming a right that we do not have.

HOW SHOULD WE RENDER A BLESSING?

"This is all fine and good," you say, "but it seems somewhat theoretical. Specifically how do I go about doing this?" Fortunately the apostle Peter sets before us the supreme illustration possible, the example of the Lord Jesus Christ.

Here was a man who more than any of us was unjustly insulted. If anyone should have a justifiable basis for anger, revenge, or fear, it was the Lord Jesus. Peter tells us that we should "follow His steps" (1 Pet. 2:21). He then delineates four steps followed by the Lord Jesus in responding with a blessing. Then we read, "Likewise you wives, be submissive to your own husbands" (1 Pet. 3:1), and "Likewise you husbands, dwell with them with understanding" (1 Pet. 3:7). As Christ lived and responded, husbands and wives are to live and respond. Let's look at the steps of Christ.

Step 1. *We are to have no sin.*

For to this you were called, because
Christ also suffered for us, leaving us an
example, that you should follow His steps:
"Who committed no sin,

Nor was guile found in His mouth" (1 Pet. 2:21–22).

As Jesus Christ went through those six trials, He was mocked, scourged, and ridiculed. He was unjustly criticized and condemned. If ever a man had reason to explode in anger and bitterness, He had it. None of us has ever suffered as He suffered. While it is true that He was sinless, this only made His temptation greater. All of us when we sin yield before the final strain. Because Jesus Christ was unable to sin, He had to endure each temptation to anger, to bitterness, to fear to the uttermost before it departed. So His temptation to sin in these areas was even greater.

Yet He was sinless, and so we are to be. It is extremely difficult when we have been offended not to respond with anger or bitterness. So the first step in a proper response is to examine our own hearts. First of all, this will involve confession of any sin in our hearts toward God:

> If we confess our sins, He is faithful and just to forgive us our sins and to cleanse us from all unrighteousness. If we say that we have not sinned, we make Him a liar, and His word is not in us (1 John 1:9–10).

But, second, it may be necessary to ask forgiveness of those who are actually offending us. We must examine our hearts to explore if there is any reason in us that has provoked the offense. If there is, our first responsibility is to ask forgiveness (see Matt. 5:23–24).

Step 2. *We are to purpose to render a blessing for the insult or hurt we have experienced.*

Now comes the moment for decision of the will. "When He was reviled, [He] did not revile in return; when He suffered, He did not threaten" (1 Pet. 2:23). Each of us might think through some questions: What positive qualities about my husband can I praise him for? What benefits could I bestow upon him? In what way can I be a blessing to him? What qualities about my husband am I thankful for, and how can I communicate this to him? What specific areas of my husband's life should I pray that the Lord will bless him in?

The Lord Jesus did not retaliate when He suffered or was insulted. Sometimes in the middle of a hurtful situation, it is best to keep silent. The apostle James gives similar counsel when he says, "Therefore, my beloved brethren, let every man be swift to hear, slow to speak, slow to wrath" (James 1:19). If you are in the midst of a hurtful situation and you find anger and bitterness welling up inside you, it may be wise to heed the words of Solomon:

> He who guards his mouth preserves his life,
> But he who opens wide his lips shall have destruction (Prov. 13:3).

> A wholesome tongue is a tree of life,
> But perverseness in it breaks the spirit (Prov. 15:4).

Peter tells us only what Jesus didn't do: He didn't respond with an insult. We know from the Gospels, of course, what He did do. He responded with a blessing. He said, "Father, forgive them. They know not what they do," (see Luke 23:34). And then He died for the sins of the world.

Step 3. *We are to commit ourselves and the situation to the Lord.*

As we examine more closely this magnificent illustration of faith, we read, "[He] committed Himself to Him who judges righteously" (1 Pet. 2:23). Instead of retaliating as He knew He could, He trusted the situation to the Lord. He knew the truth of Romans 12:19, "Vengeance is Mine." Christ knew that it was His responsibility to make godly responses and that it was the Father's responsibility to deal with those who offended.

Practically speaking, how do we commit ourselves and the situation to the Lord? Despite the number of books written on this subject and the new insights, after twenty-three years of walking with the Lord, I know of no more significant response than the one I was taught the first year I became a Christian. Let's begin with Romans 8:28: "All things work together for good." In view of that tremendous promise, we are commanded by God to give thanks, not for the situation but for the good that will come out of it. Then, second, we must commit ourselves to the Lord's keeping and vow to withdraw from the battle, so the Lord can begin to deal with the offenders. We must release the Lord to act.

Step 4. *We are to purpose to be willing to suffer in order to heal.*

We are now approaching the inner sanctum of the meaning of Christ's death. In His love for us, His sacrifice was so great, so total, so complete that He was willing to suffer that we might be healed: "[He] Himself bore our sins in His own body on the tree, that we, having died to sins, might live for righteousness—by whose stripes you were healed" (1 Pet. 2:24).

This was a profound act of self-sacrifice and one that the apostle holds up to use for an example. Then he says, "Wives, in the same way be submissive to your husbands so that, if any of them do not believe the word, they may be won over without talk by the behavior of their wives" (1 Pet. 3:1 NIV). It seems that God is saying, "Wives, look at the example of My Son. He suffered to heal all men. In His suffering, He did not sin; He did not retaliate; He did entrust Himself to Him who judges righteously. In so doing, He brought about your salvation. Wives, let My Son be your example—you, too, may have the privilege to live a godly life before your husband that he might be changed and healed." Is it easy to follow Christ's example? No. Is it worth it? Yes.

I would like to share a very personal illustration from our marriage, which I did not relate in the first edition of this book. I'm doing so now only because my husband insists that it would be helpful to many readers. The events in question transpired eighteen years ago so they are history, but God has used them significantly in both our lives.

Jody and I became Christians when we were university students. Jody had lived a typical wild fraternity lifestyle while majoring in electrical engineering at Oregon State University and had rejected the church. When he became a Christian, he experienced a radical change in his entire life and personality. He embraced a new value system, and he became an extremely vibrant witness for Christ. However, the shock to the system of someone going through such a radical transformation sometimes takes years to absorb.

In the early years of our marriage, Jody struggled severely with depression, generally brought on by his perceived inability to live up to the standards God requires in Scripture. These depressions were extremely severe, and perhaps three times a month he basically would become psychologically immobile and would retreat from reality for as much as thirty-six hours at a time. Sometimes during these periods of gloom, he would make cutting comments toward me, which he did not really mean but which hurt me deeply. I can remember thinking during the first year of our marriage, *What have I done marrying this man?* I had to make some very fundamental decisions about my commitment to Jody and my commitment to the Lord, and I decided that as God enabled me I would respond with a blessing and restrain my tongue. I purposed in my heart to unconditionally love and accept and bring healing to this man I loved and to whom I had committed my life. The progress was gradual but steady. Over a period of about four years, a complete transformation occurred.

As Jody looked at my unconditional acceptance, he began to get a clearer picture of God's unconditional acceptance of us, even though we are not perfect. Second, he told me he was impressed by the fact that I assumed responsibility for the situation whereas he felt that some of his depression was a result of not assuming responsibility for his emotions. Finally, I learned a lot about unconditional love and acceptance. Even though this was a painful time, God turned it into a beautiful experience.

Peter holds out the hope for which we should all pray: "For you were like sheep going astray, but have now returned to the Shepherd and Overseer of your souls" (1 Pet. 2:25). The Lord Jesus suffered in order to heal. This is the challenge that Peter sets before us as wives. Are you willing to suffer in order to bring about healing in the life of your husband?

The principle of responding with a blessing has become a very significant part of Jody's life and my life, not only in our marriage but with our children and with our relationships in general. We have discovered that Peter was right. When we return a blessing for an insult, we do inherit a blessing!

◄ 9 ►

My Beloved and My Friend

During a seminar in Missouri, I told the women we were going to discuss being creative lovers, and one woman said quite loudly, "Whoopee!" I hope you, too, are as eager to learn about this important area of your marriage!

Today, we are all bombarded with the world's view of sex. In fact, we can't miss it! What many of us are missing is God's view of sex. And He has many interesting things to say on the subject. The Bible discusses sex openly and matter-of-factly, considering it a precious gift from God. Each of us has ideas, opinions, fears, frustrations, and inhibitions that have accumulated over our lifetimes. Romans 12:2 says, "Do not be conformed to this world, but be transformed by the renewing of your mind." Stop right now and ask God to give you a clean mental slate. He will help you put aside all preconceived ideas. Only then will you be ready to hear what He has to say. God wants to renew your minds in every area, including sexual attitudes.

EXCHANGING GIFTS

Let the husband render to his wife the affection due her, and likewise also the wife to her husband. The wife does not have authority over her own body, but the husband does. And likewise the husband does not have authority over his own body, but the wife does. Do not deprive one another except with consent for a time, that you may give yourselves to fasting and prayer; and come together again so that Satan does not tempt you because of your lack of self-control (1 Cor. 7:3–5).

Here Paul says that your body is a gift to your husband and his body is a gift to you. In a sense, he is saying that a husband and a wife should be totally available to each other. He also says, "Stop depriving each other, except to devote yourself to prayer." (My husband says he has heard of women giving many excuses to avoid sex, but never prayer!)

This passage from 1 Corinthians shows the equality God wants in the sexual relationship. A wife may have been taught a distorted concept of women's sexual nature. She may have been told that a woman "by nature" has less sexual drive than a man, is less passionate, is less frequently and intensely aroused, and that strong sexual desire and satisfaction are not parts of her nature.

Certainly men and women differ in their sexual responses, just as they differ in anatomy and physiology. But the pleasure and satisfaction experienced by a wife, while different from that of her husband, is at least as deep and profound. Her sex drive is also equally strong. If, in fact, we could compare the magnitude of response, there are a number of reasons we might expect to find her drive stronger and her satisfaction greater. "The sexual vigor of a healthy, erotically awakened woman is very great; in fact, it may be greater than the potency of the average man."[1]

GET INTOXICATED

> Drink from your own well, my son—be faithful and
> true to your wife. Let your manhood be a blessing;
> rejoice in the wife of your youth. Let her charms
> and tender embrace satisfy you. Let her love alone
> fill you with delight (Prov. 5:15, 18–19 TLB).

A beautiful parallel is drawn here between thirst being quenched by drinks of cool, fresh water and a couple's sexual thirst being satisfied by regular, exciting
sexual union in marriage.

The phrase "rejoice in the wife of your youth" indicates that the sexual relationship is to provide the marriage partners great pleasure. The wife is described as
tender, charming, loving, and satisfying.

My favorite translation of this passage is, "Let your
love and your sexual embrace with your wife *intoxicate*
you continually with delight. Always enjoy the *ecstasy*
of her love." What a picture! I fail to see here the poor,
enduring wife who puts up with her husband's sexual
advances. I see an exciting, highly erotic, and loving
relationship. Since this picture of marriage is from God's
Word, it's a good bet that this is what He has in mind
for your marriage.

SOLOMON'S BEST SONG

The Song of Solomon contains eight chapters of beautiful poetry, picturing the love relationship between
husband and wife. It describes in vivid, poetic language
the physical bodies of married lovers, techniques in
sexual arousal between husband and wife, the feelings,
the attitudes, the imaginations, the dreams, and the

spiritual and sexual joys they experience.[2] (For a better understanding of the Song of Solomon, read my husband's excellent book *Solomon on Sex* [Thomas Nelson, 1977].)

Solomon's Song is the story of the king of Israel, who wooed and won the Shulamite, a lovely country maiden, as his wife. Each passage is packed with abundant lessons from God on the sexual aspects of marriage.

COMPLIMENTS AND OTHER GOODIES

"Like an apple tree among the trees of the woods, / So is my beloved among the sons" (Song of Sol. 2:3). Solomon and his bride are actively involved in lovemaking in this passage. Since the apple is a very frequent symbol in the Near East for love, it is used throughout the Song to symbolize sexual love. She is telling him what a fantastic lover he is.

You may not think of your husband as the last of the red-hot lovers, but he wants you to! A man's ego is intricately tied up in his ability as a lover, and your rejection can scar him deeply. We have the idea that women are the sensitive ones, but I believe men are more sensitive when it comes to sex. If you think he is a boring, run-of-the-mill lover, that's probably just what he'll be. He needs and wants to hear your praise. Tell him that you find his body attractive, that his desire to please you is exciting, and that you like the way his hands are so gentle and yet so strong. Every man longs to hear, "Honey, you're a fantastic lover!" Or "I feel sorry for every other woman in the world because they don't have you for a lover!"

Perhaps you're thinking, *Oh, brother! There is absolutely nothing sexy about that guy I'm married to!* Oh, yes, there is. There is always *something* you can praise him for. Never be deceptive, but creatively search for the positive qualities. Verbalize your praise. He'll love it!

STATE YOUR PREFERENCE

Solomon and his bride continue with their lovemaking. She says, "Sustain me with cakes of raisins, / Refresh me with apples, / For I am lovesick" (2:5).

By saying she is sick or weak with love, she means she is completely overcome with sexual desire. She therefore asks Solomon to sustain her with raisin cakes and apples (symbols of erotic love). In other words, she is asking him to satisfy her sexually without delay!

Solomon's wife then tells him exactly how he satisfies her: "His left hand is under my head, / And his right hand embraces me" (2:6). This suggests that she desires him to fondle and stimulate her body. Please take note! They are communicating during their lovemaking— openly, unashamedly, and freely. Solomon explains what he is doing to please her and asks what else he can do to satisfy her. Often a husband and a wife don't know how to please each other because they have what I call "silent sex."

A woman came in for counseling and said that after twenty years of marriage she had never experienced an orgasm. The counselor asked if she had ever told her husband how to stimulate her. She said, "Oh, of course not."

LOOK IN THE MIRROR

In chapter 4 of the Song of Solomon is the second love scene. Solomon praises his wife's physical appearance, starting at the top and working downward, probably caressing her as he speaks. He says she has eyes like a dove's; her hair is long and black; her teeth, smooth and white; her lips, red and lovely; her cheeks, fair; her neck, erect; her breasts, full and youthful; her garden (genitals), erotically scented.

Throughout the Song of Solomon, poetic language is used to describe the genitalia. The "garden" refers to the female genitals and the "fruit" to the male genitals.

What is your husband's picture of you? Is he aware of your femininity? Does he think of you as an exciting woman and his lover, or are you just his children's mother and his housekeeper? Does he consider you attractive? It's a tragedy when a woman stops caring about her personal appearance. Let's get personal. Do *you* care as much *now* about your appearance as you did before you were married?

I have a friend whose husband is a pilot, and he is often home for days at a time. One morning she went into the bathroom about nine and spent an hour taking a shower, shaving her legs, powdering, perfuming, dressing, and fixing her hair. She walked into the living room, and her husband asked, "Where are you going?" When she told him she had her yearly appointment with her gynecologist, he said, "Gosh. I wish you'd get dressed up like that for me sometimes!"

Because she is embarrassed about going to the gynecologist, she grooms herself perfectly from head to toe in order to compensate. (I'm sure a survey of doctors would reveal that they rarely see a woman with unshaved legs!) It's a sad irony that a wife may dress up for a comparative stranger but look like a washerwoman for her husband.

Do you seek by your physical appearance to please your husband? I found out after several years of marriage that Jody wasn't wild about my abundance of red, white, and blue outfits. He likes very bright colors and pastels. So who do I dress to please, the editors of *Harper's Bazaar* or my husband?

Jody likes thin women—a problem for me since I love to eat! My view of heaven is a banquet table with delicacies available continuously. Because of this, through blood, sweat, tears, and Weight Watchers, I lost twenty pounds! Recently Jody put his arms around me and said, "Honey, I love your new body."

One wise woman told me she always freshens her makeup and hair and, if necessary, changes her clothes before her husband arrives home. "After all," she said, "he looks at women who strive to be attractive all day at the office. Shouldn't I try as hard?"

I've asked Jody to call me before he leaves work, so I have fifteen minutes to prepare myself physically, emotionally, and spiritually. Of course he doesn't always remember, but when he does, I have time to again give my day to God, asking Him to help me get my eyes off myself and onto Jody. I ask God to make me sensitive to Jody's needs and to how I can meet them when he walks in the door. Sure, I share all the joys and frustrations of my day with Jody, but first I try to concentrate on him, saving my needs for later.

EXCUSES, EXCUSES

In chapter 5, Solomon comes to his wife late at night, eager to make love, and she gives the great-granddaddy of all excuses. She says, "I have taken off my robe; / How can I put it on again?" (5:3a). This indicates that she is undressed and ready for bed and that, according to the custom, the door is already locked. In order to unlock the door and let Solomon in, she would have to get up, put on a robe, and walk across the room. In effect she's saying, "Oh, Solomon, can't it wait? Can't you see I'm tired and all ready for bed?"

Then she comes up with another excuse: "I have washed my feet, how can I dirty them again?" (see 5:3b). Since it was a religious ritual to wash one's feet before going to bed, she is saying, "Not only would I have to put on my robe and walk across the room, but I'd even have to rewash my feet!"

How do you respond to your husband's lovemaking? Do you respond with eagerness, joy, and tenderness, or do you avoid it as often as possible and endure it when you have to? Are any of these excuses familiar?

- Sudden headache.
- Too tired. (You *are* tired! You've been doing things for people all day, and now you want to crawl under the sheets and be left alone!)
- Saying no as punishment. Is sex a favor you bestow or withhold according to whether or not you are pleased with him?

Are you remembering past wrongs? Has he been unfaithful, and that keeps coming back to your mind each time he wants to give love to you? I don't mean to minimize the hurt and anguish a wife feels if her husband has been unfaithful, but if you dwell on it, you'll destroy yourself and your marriage.

Apply 1 Corinthians 13 to your sexual relationship. Is it patient and kind? Is it never envious or jealous? Is it not possessive, not conceited or rude, never indiscreet? Does it not insist on its own way? Is it not self-seeking, never touchy or resentful? Does it pay no attention to a suffered wrong? Does it not count up past wrongs, but always believes the best of him? Does it never fail?

We are not capable of that kind of love by ourselves. But with God all things are possible. God is at work within us every day, conforming us to the image of Christ.

If a wife continually makes excuses to avoid her husband physically, four things are likely to happen in her marriage.

1. *Her husband will react.* He may try slight pressure at first, then apply force, causing terrible problems in the relationship. After putting up with countless excuses, one husband finally confronted his wife, "You are a good mother, a good cook, and a good housekeeper. You're attractive and socially poised. But, Baby, I need a woman!" With that statement, he walked out the door for the last time.

2. *Her husband will let her have her way, silently resenting her.* The relationship will suffer disastrous consequences. One wife said, "My husband leaves me alone. He only approaches me once a month, and that's the way I like it."

What kind of love relationship is that? What kind of marriage is it when both partners avoid each other for fear of a fight over sex? The wife sleeps on one side of the bed and the husband on the other, hoping their big toes never touch because the other might think it was a sexual advance! This is not a marriage at all. It's two strangers occupying the same dwelling.

3. *She'll tempt him to adultery.* If she has shattered his ego by constant refusal or has played the "dutiful wife" who endures him sexually, she has left him open to the sweetness and tenderness of another woman. To prove to himself that he is attractive and desirable as a man, he might seek out a woman who will make him feel loved. If he commits adultery under these circumstances, the wife is also guilty.

4. *She'll be out of fellowship with God.* The Bible says clearly that a wife does not have authority over her own body in marriage but that her husband does. The same is true of his body. If either partner has usurped that authority, God has been disobeyed.

DELIGHTFUL DAYDREAMING

Solomon's wife describes her husband physically:

> My beloved is white and ruddy,
> Chief among ten thousand.
> His head is like the finest gold;
> His locks are wavy,
> And black as a raven.
> His eyes are like doves
> By the rivers of waters,
> Washed with milk,
> And fitly set.
> His cheeks are like a bed of spices,
> Like banks of scented herbs.
> His lips are lilies,
> Dripping liquid myrrh.
> His hands are rods of gold
> Set with beryl.
> His body is carved ivory
> Inlaid with sapphires.

His legs are pillars of marble
Set on bases of fine gold.
His countenance is like Lebanon,
Excellent as the cedars.
His mouth is most sweet,
Yes, he is altogether lovely.
This is my beloved,
And this is my friend (Song of Sol. 5:10–16).

Solomon is not present. His wife is daydreaming about her husband, her lover and friend. What a perfect combination! She pictures him in her mind and concludes he is wholly desirable. Her thoughts of him are very physical, and she anticipates his return.

How do you think about your husband? Is he that nice man who brings home the paycheck, goes to church, and plays with the children? That's fine, but it's not enough! Think back. How did you think of him before you were married? I'm sure you noticed and thought about his physique—his strong hands and how good it felt when he put his arms around you. You noticed the straightness of his shoulders, the smile that told you he longed to have you as his own. It sent chills up your spine. After you live with someone for several years, however, you stop noticing. In fact, a wife may notice only the *bad* things and tease her husband about his potbelly and receding hairline.

I'll never forget an experience I had at a university where I had been invited to speak to a group of young women. I enjoyed a luncheon with them, and when I was introduced as Linda Dillow, a cute little eighteen year old piped up and said, "Oh, are you Jody Dillow's wife? I think he's wonderful!" The last sentence was said with a sort of swoon. She went on to talk about my husband as if he were Tarzan, Albert Einstein, and Billy Graham all in one.

I barely made it through my message that afternoon. All the way home I thought about the way this girl saw my husband. It jolted me to look at him through another woman's eyes!

How does your husband's secretary see him? A wife should see her husband across the room and smile inside that she knows him as no one else does. Other women can look and admire, but he is hers to possess. One writer has suggested that a wife should have a "holy lust" for her husband. The word *lust* is used carefully, meaning "a strong desire to possess or enjoy." There is a difference in being possessive and possessing! The desire to know all there is to know of your husband, to own him completely, and to be totally possessed of him sexually is not being possessive.[3]

Are you in love with your husband? Oh, I know you love him. He's been around a long time, and you're used to him. Are you *in love* with him? How long has it been since your heart throbbed when you looked at him? Everyone hates to be taken for granted. Your husband needs to be told that you love him and that he is attractive to you. Tonight, get your eyes off the dirty dishes long enough to really look at him. Then open your mouth (pry it open, if necessary) and tell him you love him and desire him.

LET YOURSELF GO!

In the scene depicted in chapter 6, Solomon and his wife are alone in the palace. She desires to make love with her husband and aggressively takes the initiative. As part of their loveplay, and as her way of arousing his sexual interest, she dances nude before him. As she dances, she coyly says to him, "Why would you gaze on the Shulammite, as on the dance of Mahanaim?" (v. 13 NIV). (The dance of the Mahanaim contained movements as magnificent and transporting as the dance of an angel, and as sensuous as the Near Eastern dancer.) It seems rather obvious why he was gazing at her!

Solomon replies, "How beautiful your sandaled feet, O prince's daughter! / Your graceful legs are like jewels, the work of a craftsman's hands" (7:1 NIV).

In case you didn't know, men are aroused by the sight of the female body. Because the world exploits this to the extreme and misuses the body, a wife may feel she should do the opposite of the world. If the world exposes the body, she will conceal it. She is not going to be like those nasty women in the *Playboy* centerfold!

I am disgusted by the blatant exploitation of sex. Recently while searching the theater section of the newspaper to find a good movie, I was sickened at the multitude of X-rated movie advertisements. They infuriate me because they degrade God's gift and cheapen it.

We glorify God in our bodies not only by abstaining from the improper use of sex but also by enjoying the proper and holy use of our bodies in the sexual relationship. The world is wrong to expose the body, but a wife is just as wrong to conceal her body from her husband. God's Word says that a husband and a wife are to delight in and be aroused by the sight of the other's body. God created a husband to be aroused by his wife's body!

Why doesn't a wife provocatively display her body?

1. *She has too many inhibitions.* Everyone has at least a few—and they're crippling to a healthy marriage. We'll deal with this problem in detail in the next chapter.

2. *She doesn't like her body.* One wife told me she didn't like her husband to see her without clothing because she was sure he was looking at the roll around her middle!

There are many things about our bodies we cannot change, but there are many we can. Weight is one of them. I wish I knew of a superdiet so that all you'd have to do is pray and the pounds would fall off! I struggle constantly with my weight and know that when I am slender I feel much better about myself and feel much more attractive to my husband. If you need to lose weight, do it! If you need to exercise, do it! You can spend the rest of your life "wishing" you liked your figure. I've found dieting one of the best ways to learn more self-control. Since self-control is part of the fruit of the Spirit (see Gal. 5:22–23), you should actively desire it. You'll get a double bonus—lose weight and become more spiritual at the same time.

Solomon continues to praise his wife as she dances, and he says, "I will climb the palm tree; I will take hold of its fruit" (7:8 NIV). To climb the palm tree is to fertilize it. Solomon is saying he intends to make love to his wife.

Then his wife says, "I belong to my lover, and his desire is for me" (7:10 NIV). She expresses that she is totally his and available to please him. She thrills in the fact that Solomon desires her physically.

God's picture of marriage, painted in Scripture, describes a beautifully satisfying and free relationship. I pray that these few passages have shown you what God has in mind for every Christian marriage. When He tells you to enjoy sex freely and *joyfully* with your husband, He means *get after it!*

❧ 10 ❧

The Creative Lover

BREAKING THE RESPONSE BARRIER

God's picture of marriage as a beautifully satisfying and free sexual relationship is never realized in many marriages. Couples who do not experience this unifying physical oneness are unable to respond. For a man, this could mean impotence (the inability to have an erection) or premature ejaculation (an orgasm occurring immediately or shortly after entry). For a woman, the inability to respond usually results in the inability to have an orgasm. For some women, however, it means the inability to feel at all sexually. And for others, it means a total lack of interest in the sexual relationship.

CAUSES OF A LACK OF RESPONSE

GOAL ORIENTATION

Often, when a woman has difficulty responding sexually, it is because she fears she won't have an orgasm. The goal of the sexual union becomes the female orgasm; or for a man, overcoming impotence. In contrast to this, the goal of sexual union should be the giving and receiving of love.

A wife who has been unable to achieve orgasm focuses on this failure. She begins to dread every lovemaking time because she is afraid she will fail once again. Herbert J. Miles described this pattern in *Sexual Happiness in Marriage:*

> A wife who has not achieved sexual orgasm is usually in an unfortunate situation. In her sexual experiences with her husband, she is sometimes slightly aroused, but never satisfied.
>
> Secretly she is disappointed but does not admit it. Sexually, she had expected much in marriage, and rightly so, but she has received little. She is careful to meet her husband's sexual needs, but secretly wonders if there is something wrong with her. As the weeks pass into months, and the months pass into years, the same pattern prevails—slightly aroused, but never satisfied. Gradually she becomes nervous, and irritable. The experience becomes distasteful to her. She puts it off as long as possible.[1]

It is important for a woman to achieve orgasm regularly, yet this should not be the goal of the sexual union. A wife can be a skillful and exciting lover to her husband even if she never has an orgasm. If she relaxes and enjoys loving her husband and being loved by him, there is a much greater probability that she will learn to achieve orgasm.

THE SPECTATOR ROLE

One of the most damaging barriers to sexual stimulation is playing the role of spectator in the sexual union. Instead of getting involved, instead of forgetting everything else and letting sexual arousal happen naturally, a person may adopt this role because of the fear of failing to respond. Mentally the self is set aside, and the person "watches" to see if a response will occur. Because there is no involvement, the individual cannot respond, thus beginning a vicious cycle of hoping, "watching," and failing.

IT'S ALL HIS FAULT!

A wife may blame her husband for her own lack of response. Perhaps it's his sexual approach: "Do you wanna do it?" Or perhaps she feels if her husband knew more about sex or were more tender, or less gross, or more anything, *then* she would be able to respond.

Certainly husbands need to learn and grow in the area of sex just as wives do! However, I'm convinced that most women have the *ability* to respond if they want to. Much of a woman's response (or lack of it) is centered in her will and her mind. A wife may need to look at her own weaknesses instead of majoring on those of her husband, and she may need to realize that a major hindrance to sexual adjustment in marriage is the lack of time for sexual experience. Many couples hurry through life and through their sexual experiences.

LOOKING TOWARD RESPONSE

GET THE FACTS

I have been amazed at how uninformed many people are about sexual matters! Often a man and a woman marry, each thinking the other is knowledgeable about the sexual relationship, when in reality they both lack even the most basic facts! I have talked to bright, intelligent young women who did not know (for the first several years of marriage) that a woman could or should experience an orgasm. We need to learn all we can. I believe a married couple should read at least one new book a year about the physical relationship. The list of books at the end of this chapter is a good place to start.

SURRENDER TO YOUR ROLE

Examine yourself first. What is your attitude toward manhood and womanhood? Do you resent the man's role and wish it were yours, or are you excited about your role as a woman and about being a *creative counterpart* to your husband?

I wish you could meet Janice. As a sharp, competitive businesswoman with a colossal salary, she is capable, deadly efficient, and strong. My friendship with her began as I was preparing to give my first Creative Counterpart Seminar. Janice approached me coolly and said, "I'm coming to your seminar Wednesday, and it had better be good. This will be the first time I've taken off from work in twelve years. You had better be studying." Her whole manner said, in essence, "Just try to teach me something. I dare you!"

Arriving at the seminar before the doors were open, Janice was ready for the attack. I could sense her challenging spirit and tried not to look at her as I spoke. After the concluding message, she waited to speak with me. She said, "I'm going to give you the greatest compliment I have ever given a woman. I wish I could trade brains with you. For thirty-three years I have believed exactly the opposite of everything you said today, and I see how terribly wrong I have been. I am determined to change. So watch out, Linda Dillow, because in one week I will be more submissive than you are!"

The change hit her household like a bombshell. Her husband, who had always followed her, began to take the lead. Her children, who had disliked her as a person, grew to adore her. And Janice herself, always a unique person, became a godly one. She had told me after the seminar that she was starting at minus ten—and she was! Soon, however, the minus changed to a plus, and the change was so great that friends visiting in her home said she was a totally different person!

Janice told me later that she had always resented being a woman. She was as smart as most men and smarter than many! Janice changed as she surrendered to the role for which God had created her. She even surprised herself because she loved it. The changes permeated into every area of her life and marriage, even into her sexual relationship with her husband.

We became close friends, and one evening as we were chatting she said, "Linda, there is one aspect of my marriage I have never shared with you. Despite my leading and running the family, we had a good marriage, except in the area of our sexual relationship. During our entire thirteen years of marriage, I was unable to have an orgasm, and this greatly disturbed my husband. Since we are wealthy and could do so, we traveled to twenty states seeking help. We saw gynecologists, psychiatrists, and sex doctors. I had my head shrunk, my body shrunk, even had an operation, and yet nothing changed.

"One week after attending your seminar and yielding to all God wanted me to be, I experienced an orgasm. My husband was so excited he paced the floor most of the night saying, 'I don't believe it!' "

Some of you may carry resentments as Janice did. Ask God right now for the proper attitude. Begin to focus on all God wants you to be as a woman. Surrender to your role as a *creative helpmate* to your husband, to all we have discussed in this book about the role of the wife.

View your husband with new eyes! Ask God to let you see him anew. If you have not experienced an orgasm, or do so rarely, release this as the ultimate goal of your sexual union. Instead, love your husband and enjoy learning what pleases you sexually. God will take care of the results!

OPEN LINE TO YOUR HUSBAND

God wants you and your husband to communicate openly and freely in every area of your relationship, including sex. Perhaps you could read the Song of Solomon together from The Living Bible, or you could share your thoughts after reading some of the books or listening to the tapes on the sexual relationship I have listed at the end of this chapter. I cannot stress enough the importance of communication in this area. Probably 50 percent of all sexual problems can be solved by open, honest, and loving communication.

YOU SHALL OVERCOME

In a survey taken of five hundred Christian men and women, 40 percent of the women said the biggest problem for them in the physical relationship was that they were too inhibited. As I talk and counsel with women, I discover this same problem again and again. Inhibitions can be crippling! We must overcome them! I have had the privilege of sharing the following steps toward overcoming inhibitions with hundreds of women who have profited from them. I pray they will be helpful to you, too!

1. *Renew your mind.* Your ideas about sex may differ from what God had in mind. He wants you to realize and put into practice the glorious picture He paints of marriage in the Song of Solomon. Reread it, and ask God to give you His attitude. Saturate your mind with all available information on the beautiful, free, sexual relationship God has given a husband and wife.

2. *Memorize and meditate on God's viewpoint.* God says that His Word is like a two-edged sword, piercing into our lives. For years you have had at least some negative thoughts and feelings about sex, and God wants to change all that through His Word.

A woman came to me for counseling and expressed concern about the inhibitions that kept her from being the creative lover she wanted to be. We talked about many things during our time together, but at the top of the list I suggested memorizing passages from Scripture such as 1 Corinthians 7, Proverb 5, and the Song of Solomon. Knowing what a fantastic effect God's Word has on the situation it addresses (and fearing she might not do the memory work), I told her I would call her the following Tuesday so she could repeat her verses to me. I proceeded to write in my *Priority Planner* for that day, "Call Marilyn." She knew me well enough to know I do everything written in my planner like a robot!

I called Marilyn the following Tuesday, and the first thing she said was, "Do you have a cup of coffee?" Coffee in hand, I sat down to listen as she repeated ten to fifteen verses from memory! When I asked if it had helped, she replied she could hardly believe the difference.

"Throughout the day, I memorized and meditated on the Scriptures and found that I had an excited anticipation about our sexual relationship," she said. "During lovemaking, when negative thoughts would come, I would think about the passages I had learned and found that the tension would leave. At this rate, I just might memorize the whole Song of Solomon!"

3. *Decide with your will to be God's version of a creative lover.* So much of change starts with a decision. All change is hard and much of it takes time, but you can't begin until you decide, "Yes, God. I want to do it Your way."

Jane had a crummy marriage and an even crummier view of sex. Sex was animalistic, in her opinion, and she wanted little to do with it. Her husband was not a Christian, and because she considered sex with him as only physical, she rejected him. She came to me wanting me to agree with her view; needless to say, I didn't. As we talked together, I shared God's view of the sexual relationship and encouraged her to decide to be God's version of a creative lover. Because she lived in another state, I doubted if I would ever know the outcome.

One year later I was speaking in her city, and she walked into the room. Her appearance was so changed that I hardly recognized her. There was a softness about her, a new quality of happiness and peace. Coming up to me, she said, "Linda, you won't believe what happened." I said I'd believe anything because I could see it in her face. Out poured a story of two people married over twenty-five years who had learned anew to love each other, to touch each other, and to care.

She talked on and told me of her first attempt at a weekend away. "I took him out to dinner and had reservations at the motel across the street. All he talked about during dinner was the movie on TV that night. I was sure my plans were to end in disaster, and we would watch the tube all night. Not exactly what I had planned. And Linda, would you believe that just as we left the restaurant the electricity for the entire block went out and stayed out until after the ten o'clock news! We went to our motel room by candlelight, and we had no lights or TV set all evening!" She went on to tell me that her nineteen-year-old daughter had told her she had never seen a marriage she would want, especially her mother and father's. Jane told me, "Linda, by God's grace, it will be our marriage she will want!" God is so gracious. He even turned off electricity when needed!

4. *Do your part—your 100 percent.* In the early years of our marriage, Jody asked me to tell him in detail everything I wanted him to do to please me sexually and then to tell him everything I was going to do to please him. I said (gulp!), "In detail?" I was totally embarrassed. I could barely think such things, much less verbalize them! I knew, however, that I could claim embarrassment and refuse to tell him or swallow my self-consciousness and tell him freely how I was going to love him. It was embarrassing the first time, but later my bashfulness grew less and finally faded completely.

I have met many women who claim "embarrassment." A wife may feel that in a year or two she will be more ready to respond as her husband would like. That may be true in some cases, but it seems to me that the longer she waits, the harder it will be to overcome her embarrassment.

After making the decision in your will to go God's

way, you must do all you can to change. God will do the rest.

5. *Give God time to work.* I have known women who, after implementing these principles, were released of their inhibitions overnight. For others, it has been a gradual process. God works individually with each of us. If you have incorporated these principles into your own relationship, you're halfway there! Now give God the Holy Spirit time to work on the inside. He specializes in changed hearts.

BREAKING THE CREATIVITY BARRIER

BE TOTALLY AVAILABLE

We read in 1 Corinthians 7:4 that we no longer have authority over our own bodies in marriage, but our husbands do. One doctor recited this verse to a female patient who was having sexual problems in her marriage. Looking at him in abject horror, she told him if she were totally available to her husband, they would never get out of bed! The wise doctor reassured the distraught patient that she and her husband wouldn't have intercourse nearly as often as she feared. "Someone who bangs on the door forty times when it stays locked," he said, "only knocks once if you open right away."

A wife who hasn't reached sexual harmony with her husband may find him making some kind of advance nearly every night. She is afraid she will be asked to participate more often than she can bear if she lets down the barriers. Actually, a man who has intercourse as often as he wants finds that in a week or two the pressure of his physical urge is relieved, and the psychological pressure to overcome resistance no longer applies. So his sex pace tapers off.

One man told my husband that his wife was available to him in spurts. "After she attends Linda's seminar or reads a book on sex or after we have a knockdown, drag-out fight about sex, she is more available and has a good attitude," he said. "I know from experience it will only last a few days. So when she is responsive, I take advantage of it. Then because I do, my wife thinks all I ever think about is sex!"

Have you ever been on a diet? (I can hear you moaning.) When you're on a diet, all you can think about is food. When you can eat all you want, however, you're not nearly so interested in food. It's the same with sex. When a man knows he will be rejected, he very likely becomes consumed with what he can't have. When a husband knows his wife is totally available, his desire will gradually level off. It may take some time, but as a husband sees that his wife is eager to love and be loved by him, the driving, insistent nature of the lovemaking will be replaced by a more relaxed, secure, and loving type.

NEVER AGAIN

A woman called me and said, "I have a problem. My husband wants to make love very often! Sometimes it's several times a day and often at two and again at four in the morning! We've had horrible fights. I've screamed at him and told him he was oversexed. Today he walked out of the house and told me to forget the whole thing. He said, 'I'll never approach you again.' Now, I'm really scared. I have heard you publicly state that your goal in life is to be a godly woman. Well, let me tell you, my goal in life is to make that man scream for mercy!" (I told her I would pray for her!) Later, she called to say she felt she was succeeding when she approached her husband sexually while he was watching TV and he said, "Please, let me finish this program first!"

She discovered she had to prove to him she was totally available by being aggressive toward him. It seems to be especially helpful for a wife to be aggressive when she is trying to convince her husband that her attitude has changed. For the first time her husband was truly satisfied.

Contrary to the popular opinion of many women, sex is not just physical to a man! When this woman was warm, responsive, and aggressive toward her husband, he felt he was *loved* and not just *endured*. His psychological needs of acceptance and love were met, and his frantic desire for sexual relations abated. He was still very active sexually, but their relationship was much improved because of her attitude.

TOTAL AVAILABILITY IS CHOOSING TO GIVE

A man told my husband that even when his wife satisfied him physically, he came away with a need. He said, "I feel she hasn't really given or enjoyed, but just put up with me. I need another sexual release again quickly, because I guess I'm longing for that total oneness and release that comes when both partners completely give of themselves. I know that if I was satisfied physically, emotionally, and spiritually I wouldn't walk around thinking about sex, wanting it and aching inside."

Picture this: you are busily making Christmas presents. The children are finally in bed, and for the first time that day you have a chance to do something you want and need to do. You are totally engrossed in your work as your husband walks in with that special gleam in his eye.

At this point you have a choice. You can say, "Oh, Honey, not tonight," or you can decide and choose to love this man God has given you. Your initial response may be "oh, no!" You can change that immediately to "oh, yes!" by an act of will. Once you are in his arms, you have more choices to make. If he is kissing you madly and you are still thinking about the Christmas gifts, it just won't work. Decide to think about loving him and ask God to fill you with genuine desire. I'm convinced that much of a woman's sexual response is in her brain! Dwell on how nice his body feels and what a privilege it is to love him, and your thoughts of the Christmas presents will fade away!

BE AGGRESSIVE!

I'm convinced that most husbands long for their wives to be more aggressive. A husband wants to know his wife longs for him just as he longs for her. In a survey of five hundred men and women, 40 percent of the men said the biggest problem for them in the sexual relationship was that their wives were not aggressive enough. As I mentioned before, 40 percent of the wives complained of their inhibitions, which is the same problem stated another way.

Some contemporary books have made suggestions for being aggressive that would cause some of you to rise up in alarm and shriek, "But that is not me!" That

THE CREATIVE LOVER 195

is precisely the reason I won't suggest how you should be aggressive with your own husband. Each of us is an individual, and each of us has a different husband. So no pat formula will work for everyone. God wants to work in innovative, exciting ways in each life. Ask God to show you some clever things you can do to make your marriage a love affair. Be willing, however, to put aside any inhibitions!

One woman who is old enough to be my mother said, "I asked God to show me 'my thing,' and after thirty years of marriage it was about time! I decided one evening, after taking a shower, to ask my husband to put cream on my back (it was winter, and you know how your skin gets dry). Then I got really brave and asked him to put cream all over my body! Well, that led to other things, and later I told him about hearing your seminar and reading your book and deciding to try something new!" Her husband's enthusiastic response was, "Honey, I hope that was chapter one because I can't wait for two, three, and four!"

If your husband is not used to this sort of thing, tread lightly! One woman, on Halloween night, put a mink coat over her nude body, ran outside, and rang the front doorbell, knowing her husband would be the one to answer the door. When he opened the door, she opened the mink coat and said, "Trick or Treat!" Her poor husband was so shocked that he fell backward and hit his head on the coffee table, resulting in a concussion!

Men are physically designed to respond to sight. Keep this in mind when considering aggressive tactics. Too often, a wife approaches her husband the way *she* likes to be approached—candles, romance, all the trimmings—and a husband approaches his wife the way he likes to be approached—more physically and directly. Get to know your husband and his preferences. If he wants the dance of the Mahanaim, then put on your dancing sandals!

I received a very special letter from the husband of a woman who attended my seminar. He and his wife were both in their fifties and had a good marriage relationship. He said, "Please keep telling women how important it is to be more aggressive with their husbands in the area of sex. My wife has always been sweet, submissive, and loving, but there has *never* been anything like what we have now!"

One woman wrote me a note, asking, "How far should I let my husband go?" (Does this remind you of high school?) My answer to her was this: I believe, from Scripture, that any way or anywhere you want to touch, kiss, fondle, and love your husband's body, or be loved yourself, is right and good in God's eyes. The limits are what is pleasurable to both of you.

BE CREATIVE!

You can become a Rembrandt in your sexual art, and you can stay at the paint-by-number stage.[2] What have you done creatively this week to make your sexual relationship exciting? In fact, what have you done creatively in your sexual relationship in the past year (or should I say ten years)?

LOCK THAT DOOR

It is impossible to be creative or available or aggressive if you fear that any moment the cherubs you thought were asleep burst through the bedroom door and say, "What are you doing?" I am amazed that many married couples fail to have a lock on the bedroom door. A lock does not mean you are rejecting your children; you are simply creating your own privacy.

We had just moved into our first home, and workmen were converting the garage into a lovely paneled office for Jody. I saw Jody call one of the workmen aside and ask him to put a strong lock on the master bedroom door. The workman looked up at me and cackled in what can only be described as a "dirty old man's laugh." I immediately decided I needed to go shopping and left the house, staying away until the "dirty old man" was gone! Be sure your bedroom has a sturdy lock—also be sure you are not around if your husband asks a workman to install it.

OUR HIDEAWAY AT HOME

Locking the bedroom door is a must, but what happens if the children can still hear through the walls? With little ones, you can rest assured they'll be asleep, but what do you do with teens who stay up later than you do? When our daughter kept knocking on the wall to tell us to stop talking so she could sleep, we decided something had to be done. If she could hear us talking, it was obvious she could hear other things! Our solution was to build a "penthouse bedroom" in the attic, a large room with an adjoining study for me. It has been indescribably wonderful to have our retreat. The four teens are on the second floor, and we're on the third with two strong doors in between. We can't hear them or their tape recorders, and they can't hear us.

Perhaps it is not possible for you to build a room,

but have you ever thought about creative alternatives to provide a "hideaway at home"? One woman had a lock put on her living room door and bought a special furry rug to throw on the floor. With candles, soft music, and a white furry rug she created a temporary hideaway. What have you done to create yours?

LUNCHEON SPECIAL

One woman complained that her children stayed up so late that she and her husband had very little time together. I asked her if she had ever invited him home for a special luncheon. I suggested she send him an invitation listing the luncheon menu, making it clear that there would be a very special dessert, and if he liked, he could have dessert first!

She called a few weeks later to say she hadn't had the courage to write the invitation yet, but had called and invited him for lunch and couldn't believe how fast he made it home!

CANDLELIGHT DINNER FOR TWO

If you have no children or small children who go to bed early, you can plan candlelight dinners after eight. You don't have to make an elaborate dinner—it can be the same spaghetti you served the children at six.

I remember well one candlelight dinner we had. I thought the children were asleep, but no such luck! Peering around the corner were two angels in white nightgowns saying, "What are you doing? Oh, what fun, can we have candles, too?" So, next morning we all had a candlelight breakfast!

One creative woman, whose husband is an airline

pilot and has a strange schedule, told me she fixes candlelight breakfasts at 5:00 A.M. before her husband leaves for a flight. She said it is very quiet, and they have a wonderful time talking, eating, and loving each other.

CREATIVE FOOTBALL

As football season approaches, most American wives shudder. This is especially true in Dallas, where there is so much football mania! One Christian friend was dreading the onslaught of the season. Before the regular games began, her husband was watching the preseason games. On one particular night, the game began very late. She knew she should go in and show an interest, but she really wanted to go to bed with a book. Instead, she forced herself into the TV room.

After watching a few minutes of the game, she decided to make the evening fun! She suggested to her husband that while the Cowboys were involved in a play, they'd watch. But as soon as the football play was over, they would start playing! They watched for a few minutes and when the play was over, he would say, "Rub my back until the next play." The next time, it was her turn, and she might say, "Kiss me until the next play!"

This went on throughout the entire game, and she said, "I didn't know football could be so much fun!" After three hours of this, they were super-ready to make love. Even football can be exciting—it depends on how creative you are!

SWEDISH MASSAGE

There is nothing as relaxing as an all-body massage. It helps you relax, gives a feeling of contentment, and is perfect as a prelude to lovemaking. Hand lotion or heated safflower oil is perfect applied with a hand vibrator. What a wonderful way to spend an evening: talking, laughing, and gently loving each other's bodies.

I LOVE AN AMBUSH

I must repeat once more the importance of weekends alone. Be creative and surprise your husband with one! Many motels have "weekend specials," which include the room and food in a package deal. But remember two key words—*plan* and *persevere!*

One rainy Friday night Jody and I were speaking together. I had planned a surprise retreat for the two of us and spent the afternoon packing the suitcase, preparing the food, and driving across town to get the key to our hideaway cabin.

As I was leaving the house, the children cried, "Mommy, we don't want you to go." I faltered but continued on. (Their crying stopped two seconds after I had gone, of course.)

After we finished speaking that evening, we walked to the car, and Jody said, "What's the suitcase for?"

I said, "I'm whisking you away to Holly Lake Ranch for the weekend."

He said, "Honey, thank you. I need that so much!" I forgot the hassle of the afternoon immediately!

It is *such* fun to sleep until noon, eat dinner at 10:00 P.M., and do whatever you want. It's a breath of fresh air to a marriage!

I have also baby-sat my friends' children so they can spend a weekend away. Often this is a reciprocal trade agreement. One day I picked up the phone and heard my dear friend Sara say, "It's not worth it; I really don't even want to go." Momentarily Sara was to deposit one of her children with me and escape alone with her husband for the weekend. I reassured her that I often experienced the same feelings. Often when making arrangements for the children, dog, cat, mail, and so on, you feel like staying home!

Two days later Sara came to get her daughter and said, "I never really believed that it was such fun to go to a motel with your husband. We have a great relationship and good communication, but what a joy to be free just to concentrate on him alone with no schedules or interruptions. It was wonderful, and we both can't wait to go again!"

OUR AUSTRIAN ALPS HIDEAWAY

For five days now, Jody and I have been hiding away in the Austrian Alps. We sit on our balcony, overlooking the snow-capped mountains and beautiful clear lake, and we revel in the quiet! No phone, no dog, no teenagers!

It's a chance for us both to write, but better yet, it's an opportunity to be alone with no one to give to but each other. Today I was thinking about what a woman said to me at a seminar seventeen years ago. I was sharing some of the concepts you've just read, and she interrupted me and laughingly said, "Oh, Linda, you've only been married five years. Just wait until you've been married twenty. It just isn't like that."

My dear friends, I'm here to tell you she was wrong! After twenty-two years of marriage, the joy, the freedom, and the intimacy only get better. And one way to keep the fires burning is to find your hideaway.

SIX HOURS AWAY

Maybe you would love to be alone for a weekend or longer with your husband, but you cannot arrange it right now. Have you ever thought about an evening at a motel? There are many nice motels for a reasonable price. You can take a picnic lunch or go out to dinner and come back to your room, plug in your popcorn popper (or whatever snacks you like), and talk and share and love all evening with no interruptions. You can leave the children with a baby sitter at six and be home by midnight!

Now some of you might not like the idea of going to a motel with your husband. I'm not quite sure why, but I know someone will complain. Just remember, I am not suggesting you do any of the things I have mentioned. These are only suggestions to get the old gray matter perking. God wants to work in the context of your personality and your relationship, but as my husband aptly puts it, "If nothing aggressive or creative appeals, maybe their personalities need a little changing!"

There are many creative things I can suggest, but you must start thinking and come up with your own. Remember, special times together are important and cannot be stressed enough, but the most important thing is *your attitude*. Does your husband know you are available and excited about him as your lover? God gave him to you as your beloved and your friend. Let him in on the secret!

Suggested Reading List

Dillow, Joseph. *Solomon on Sex*. Nashville: Thomas Nelson, 1977.

LaHaye, Tim and Beverly. *The Act of Marriage*. Grand Rapids: Zondervan, 1976.

Wheat, Ed and Gaye. *Intended for Pleasure*. Old Tappan, N.J.: Revell, 1981.

—— *Love Life for Every Married Couple*. Grand Rapids: Zondervan, 1980.

Wheat, Ed. *Sexual Problems and Sexual Techniques* (tapes). Bible Believers Cassettes, 130 North Spring Street, Springdale, AR   72764.

The Consistent Responder

The ways of a woman fathom none, from mood to mood she goes, and when a man's expecting one, another one she shows![1]

Too many of us are controlled by our emotions—by the way other people respond to us, by our circumstances, and by the way we feel about ourselves at the moment. God wants each of us to learn to be a consistent responder right now, not next month or next year.

Each of you has a different husband and different needs in your life. Some of you are very excited about all you have read and are already trusting God to do His 100 percent, while you are striving to do your 100 percent. Others of you perhaps wonder if it is possible for your marriage to ever be what it should, and you doubt if you'll succeed as a *creative counterpart*.

Follow me mentally back through the book, past sex, submission, reverence, and priorities to God's game plan. We talked about all He had done for us in the past and is now doing on a daily basis. With God, *all* things are possible! There is no temptation too great; no problem in your life or in your marriage that is too hard for God! If God is on your side, how can you fail? There are three essential ingredients in a happy marriage: (1) accept your circumstances; (2) accept your husband; and (3) accept yourself.[2] Your circumstances will fail, your husband will fail, and perhaps hardest of all, you will fail, but God will *never* fail.

THOSE UNPREDICTABLE CIRCUMSTANCES

After Jody graduated from seminary, we headed for the snow country of upstate New York to work with college students at Cornell University. Friends had rented us an old home in the country, and in we moved, with one toddler and another child coming soon. The next day I turned on the water and nothing happened! Racing across the street to the landlords, I told them the problem and requested they have it turned on again. It was then I learned there was no way to turn on the water because the house was built on a well. Being a city girl, I didn't know much about wells, but it soon became clear that when a well has no water, it has no water.

The Dillows were without water for six weeks. I gained a healthy appreciation for that precious commodity! The landlord was finally forced to drill another well. Because of our faith in Christ, he asked us to pray about it and tell him where to drill. As I gulped, Jody said, "Honey, if God can provide water for two million thirsty Jews in the desert, He can provide water for the Dillows on Snyder Hill Road."

Jody suggested a drilling site, and one of the best wells in the area was found. As a result of this, God worked in the lives of our landlords, increasing their faith, and using the whole situation to give us a new relationship with them!

During the six weeks without water, we made a daily pilgrimage to a Christian neighbor's home to take baths and do diapers. During this daily bath time, the woman and I began to talk about having an evangelistic coffee in her home. It was the beginning of an exciting ministry in this town.

God used our "no water" situation in many ways. I would meet people at the grocery store who would say, "Oh, I know who you are, those people without water." We became well known in the community and were able to share the love of God with many because of our "unfortunate circumstance."

"We know that all things work together for good to those who love God, to those who are the called according to His purpose" (Rom. 8:28). All things are not good, but God promises good will result for those who love Him and are called according to His purpose!

There are difficult circumstances in the life of every person, in every marriage. We each have a choice. When the hard times come, we can put up our fists and fight with anger and resentment, or we can give the situation to God and trust He will cause good to come out of even a bad situation. The first choice breeds discontent and frustration. The second breeds the fruit of the Spirit—love, joy, peace, patience, kindness, goodness, gentleness, and self-control.

God promises to produce godly qualities in our lives as we properly respond to trials. "We also rejoice in our sufferings, because we know that suffering produces perseverance; perseverance, character; and character, hope. And hope does not disappoint us, because God has poured out his love into our hearts by the Holy Spirit, whom he has given us" (Rom. 5:3–5 NIV). Do any of you need perseverance in your life? Or character? Or hope? I do! God has asked us to respond to trials by thanking Him!

By thanking God for the unreliable and difficult circumstances, we are saying, "God, You are the blessed Controller of all things. You are sovereign and in control. I don't understand all that is happening, but I thank You and trust You to teach me what You want me to learn, and to work it all together for good." God commands us to thank Him and is pleased when we do. "In everything give thanks; for this is the will of God in Christ Jesus for you" (1 Thess: 5:18).

Giving thanks is different from being thankful. I am thankful for my husband and four children and feel overwhelmed sometimes with gratitude for them. When I give thanks to God for a trial or difficult circumstance, it is not a *feeling* of thankfulness but a *decision* of my will to choose to trust God and thank Him in spite of my feelings.

PAUL—THE CONSISTENT RESPONDER

When Paul wrote the book of Philippians, he was in jail. How difficult it must have been for him! God had given him the responsibility of taking the gospel to all the known world, and there he sat, day after day, in a jail. What could possibly come out of this situation?

> And I want you to know this, dear brothers: Everything that has happened to me here has been a great boost in getting out the Good News concerning Christ. For everyone around here, including all the soldiers over at the barracks, knows that I am in chains simply

because I am a Christian. And because of my impris-
onment many of the Christians here seem to have
lost their fear of chains! Somehow my patience has
encouraged them and they have become more and
more bold in telling others about Christ (Phil. 1:12–
14 TLB).

Paul had been terribly beaten, was in jail for an unde-
termined length of time, and yet as he wrote to the
Philippians, the theme of joy was evident. Paul lived
not in his circumstances or under his circumstances
but above them!

I have learned to be content whatever the circumstances. I know what it is to be in need, and I know
what it is to have plenty. I have learned the secret
of being content in any and every situation. . . . I
can do everything through him who gives me strength
(Phil. 4:11–13 NIV).

God never said your personal or marriage problems
were easy, but He said He will give you the strength,
so why not thank Him for it in advance! Thank God
for your circumstances right now. Give your burdens
to Him, and He'll give you His peace in exchange.

As you begin to put what you have learned about
being a creative counterpart to work, your circumstances will fail. Maybe the first time you plan a candlelight dinner, the baby will get sick and you will hold
a baby in your arms all night instead of being in your
husband's arms as planned! Or perhaps you finally are
going on a date with your husband, and the car breaks
down, or he is unexpectedly called out on business,
or one or both of you get the flu. You have a choice:
you can react wrongly and fight the circumstances, or

you can respond correctly and trust God to work it together for good. I can almost guarantee you that your circumstances will fail, but praise God, He never does!

THOSE UNPREDICTABLE HUSBANDS

Creative Carol is all ready to begin admiring her husband. As Ken comes in from work she says, "Honey, I really thank you for your hard work to provide so well for us." Proud of herself for admiring him, she awaits his response. Whammo! Ken replies, "I know you don't mean that; you're always complaining about the long hours I work." Ken's response is not exactly what she has been hoping for.

Carol now has two choices. She can bite back with, "Just see if I ever compliment you again!" Or she can ignore the hurt and say, "Honey, you're right, I have been wrong to complain. I really am thankful and proud of you."

Perhaps one creative wife will try the dance of the Mahanaim for her husband, and he'll laugh (that would be a hard one)! The natural response is to take a step forward and hit back. ("You clod, I knew it would never work. I felt dumb doing that silly dance anyway!") The supernatural response is to step back and respond with a blessing.

"Do not repay evil with evil or insult with insult, but with blessing, because to this you were called so that you may inherit a blessing" (1 Pet. 3:9 NIV). Your husband is very human and may not always give just the response you were hoping for. God asks you to be faithful and do your 100 percent—not because of what you are going to get in return, but because you want to be a faithful servant. At the same time, though, God also said that when you return a blessing for an insult, you will inherit a blessing!

How do we give a blessing? By looking to God rather than to our husbands or our circumstances.

Elisabeth Elliot was a woman who returned a blessing for a great evil. Her husband, Jim, was one of five men who sought to bring the gospel of Christ to the Auca Indians, a very primitive tribe in South America, during the 1950s. While attempting to tell the Indians of the love of Christ, all five men were killed by the Indians they tried to help.

The natural response in such a tragic situation would be to hate, to be resentful, to seek revenge. Elisabeth Elliot did exactly the opposite. Taking her small daughter with her, she went back into the Auca tribe that killed her husband. She loved them and won them to a faith in Christ. In one book about her, there is a picture of her and her daughter standing by the river while the very men who killed her husband were being baptized. Elisabeth Elliot demonstrated a supernatural response; she gave a blessing instead of responding with evil or insult.

You probably will not be asked to do what Elisabeth Elliot had to do. But you may have to return a blessing when your husband disappoints or hurts you. Instead of stepping forward and hitting back, decide to step back and respond with a blessing. I can almost promise you that your husband will fail in some way, but be assured that God will never fail you!

THAT UNPREDICTABLE ME

As you seek to be a *creative counterpart*, your circumstances may fail, your husband may fail, and hardest of all, you will fail. We fail because we will never be perfect until we are with God.

I BLEW IT, LORD

I remember well one sunny afternoon at Southern Methodist University. I had spent three hours in a row going from sorority to sorority sharing with the girls about the virtuous wife in Proverb 31. I walked home so excited about being God's woman, anxious to see Jody and put what I had talked about for three hours into practice!

Walking through the door I stopped cold. Strewn through the house, in living color, were Jody's clothes. Beginning in the kitchen were the shoes and socks, in the living room his shirt, and the rest trailing into the bedroom. Obviously he had been in a hurry to go jogging! One look at those strewn clothes, and the virtuous wife was "out the window," replaced by me, "the angry wife." I blew up, screaming at Jody. Realizing what a hypocrite I was, I fell on the bed, sobbing. I had talked for three hours about the excellent wife, but I couldn't live it for three minutes! I was *hopeless!*

As I lay there sobbing, God reminded me I *wasn't* hopeless. When we're faithless, He remains faithful! Yes, I had blown it, but God loved me and forgave me, and He wanted me to forgive myself.

I'm convinced one of the greatest hindrances to growth in the Christian life is our refusal to forgive ourselves. We accept the fact that when we confess our sins He is faithful and just to forgive us our sin and cleanse us from all unrighteousness, but that's as far as it goes! In a sense, I think we feel we'll show God we're *really* sorry by moping and hating ourselves for awhile.

God says He takes our sin and casts it into the deepest sea (see Mic. 7:18–19), and then He puts up a "No Fishing" sign! He wants us to admit when we fail, then move on!

God has given me the privilege of instructing other women how to be creative wives, yet I still fail in every area discussed in this book. There are weeks when my priorities seem upside down and backward. Once again I re-evaluate them before God. There are times when the me that thinks my viewpoint is so right challenges all my husband says and is totally unsubmissive. Once again, I must ask God's forgiveness. Although I have seen exciting growth in my life, that does not mean I never fail. But my failures are fewer as I grow and learn to forgive myself and trust the Holy Spirit.

A STEP AT A TIME

Becoming a *creative counterpart* is a process. If you're on the road, you're headed toward the goal, and that's exciting! A great man once said, "It's not so important what a man is, as what he's becoming; for you shall be what you are now be-com-ing!"

I wish I could tell you that once you put down this book, magic will occur, and you will in one wave of the wand be a *creative counterpart*. It sounds terrific, but *God's* way is one step at a time. We are all habit-oriented creatures, and many of us have many bad habits! It takes three weeks to feel good about a new habit and six to make it our own. God says we are to discipline ourselves for the purpose of godliness (see 1 Tim. 4:7). This means we are to be *oriented* toward godliness. Our whole lives ought to be disciplined (structured, set up, organized, and running day to day) toward the goal of godliness. Becoming like Jesus Christ is a process, but it's an exciting one!

Look now at the project on page 214. I've asked you to list three areas discussed in this book in which you feel the *most* competent. Maybe it is admiration (you esteem and reverence your husband), or maybe you are already a creative lover, or perhaps your priorities have always been in order. Consider all areas including priorities, God's part/your part, acceptance, admiration, submission, sex, organization in the home, and consistent response. Be as specific as you like. You can choose a general category such as "priorities" or pick just one of the six priorities to zero in on. Write down your three most competent areas right now.

Next, list the three areas discussed in this book in which you feel the *least* competent. Maybe it's your priorities, or perhaps it's partner acceptance. (Are you a personal Holy Spirit?) Write down your three least competent areas right now. Take number one and write it on the calendar for this month. Then take number two and put it on the calendar for the following month. As you review this book, fill out your entire calendar something like this:

Areas Feel Most Competent
1. Priorities
2. Admiration
3. Children

Areas Feel Least Competent
1. Submission
2. Sex
3. Acceptance

January—Submission
February—Sex
March—Acceptance

See what you're doing? Step by step over the next year, as you do your part trusting God to do His part, you will change in twelve major areas of your life! This is not the wave of the wand but transformation of your habit patterns, some that you've had for a lifetime. If you diligently follow your chart, working on one area at a time, consider the state of the union at your house in six months—in one year!

List the three areas discussed where you feel the most competent.	List the three areas discussed where you feel the least competent.
1.	1.
2.	2.
3.	3.

January—

February—

March—

April—

May—

June—

July—

August—

September—

October—

November—

December—

I have used this method for the last few years, and it has been a tremendous encouragement to me. It's so easy to read a book like this and come away ready to try all! Then, after being overwhelmed with *all*, we end up changing none! I have seen real progress in my life as step by step I have taken one area of my life and worked on it for a month, then moved on to a new area. It is exciting and rewarding to be on the path headed toward the goal!

I pray you will be precious to Him who will *always* be faithful to do His part as you diligently do yours.

WHO CAN FIND AN EXCELLENT WIFE, A CREATIVE COUNTERPART? FOR HER WORTH IS FAR ABOVE RUBIES.

Notes

Chapter 2

1. Eugenia Price, *Woman to Woman* (Grand Rapids: Zondervan, 1959), p. 7.
2. Gordon MacDonald, *Ordering Your Private World* (Nashville: Thomas Nelson, 1984), pp. 20–25.
3. Derek Kidner, *The Proverbs* (Downers Grove: InterVarsity, 1972), p. 184.
4. Matthew Henry, *Matthew Henry's Commentary on the Whole Bible*, 2 vols. (Wilmington, Del.: Sovereign Grace Publishers, 1972), 2:578.

Chapter 4

1. Shirley Rice, *The Christian Home, A Woman's View* (Norfolk: Norfolk Christian Schools, 1972), p. 68.
2. Sally Meredith of Christian Family Life (Little Rock, Ark.) has contributed several helpful suggestions. The *Priority Planner* is also available from Thomas Nelson, Inc.
3. Daryl V. Hoole, *The Art of Homemaking* (Salt Lake City: Deseret Book Co., 1969), pp. 90–91.

Chapter 5

1. Judith Viorst, "What Is This Thing Called Love?" *Redbook Magazine* (February 1975).
2. *Family Life Today*, Regal Press (May 1976).
3. Many of these categories were first listed by Helen B. Andelin, *Fascinating Womanhood* (Santa Barbara: Pacific Press, 1965), pp. 36–37.
4. Ruth Bell Graham, *It's My Turn* (Old Tappan, N.J.: Revell, 1982), p. 74.

Chapter 6

1. Excerpt from *Hide or Seek* by Dr. James Dobson is Copyright © 1974 by Fleming H. Revell Company. Used by permission.

Chapter 7

1. The sequences outlined here in Plan A were first suggested to me by Don Meredith of Christian Family Life (Little Rock, Ark.).
2. Larry Christenson, *The Christian Family* (Minneapolis: Bethany Fellowship, 1970), p. 42.
3. *Collegiate Challenge Magazine* (Arrowhead Springs: Campus Crusade for Christ).
4. Alan Redpath, *Victorious Christian Living* (Old Tappan, N.J.: Revell, 1951), p. 166.
5. Suggested by Bill Gothard, *Institute in Basic Youth Conflicts.*

Chapter 9

1. Shirley Rice, *Physical Unity in Marriage* (Norfolk: Norfolk Christian Schools, 1973), p. 19.
2. Cf. *Solomon on Sex* by Joseph Dillow (Nashville: Thomas Nelson, 1977).
3. Rice, *Physical Unity*, p. 3.

Chapter 10

1. Herbert J. Miles, *Sexual Happiness in Marriage* (Grand Rapids: Zondervan, 1967), pp. 124–25.
2. Marabel Morgan, *The Total Woman* (Old Tappan, N.J.: Revell, 1973), p. 126.

Chapter 11

1. Gladys Seashore, *The New Me* (Minneapolis: His International Services, 1972), p. 20.
2. Jill Renich, *To Have and To Hold* (Grand Rapids: Zondervan, 1972), p. 23.

Bible Study and Project Guide

It is no doubt helpful to read the many books available concerning all you should be as a wife. Often, however, the excitement and enthusiasm of wanting to put these thoughts into practice lasts only a few days. Each of us needs to personally work through the Scriptures and try the projects suggested so that God's truth is *real* to us and *real* in our lives—not just something said in a book or seminar.

This follow-up *Bible Study and Project Guide* is designed to confirm the truths in this book by your own experience. It is an eight-week study, and it can be used individually or in a group. It is best, I feel, to study with a group of other women and interact with them. However, because of the personal nature of some of the questions, the following guidelines should be followed.

1. Do not mention or discuss your husband's faults. It is fine to discuss yours, but not your husband's. This would particularly apply under the section on learning to accept and respect your husband. You are asked to list your husband's faults and your wrong responses to them on one project. Don't share your husband's faults, but instead discuss your wrong responses and

seek help from the group about habits of nagging, your silent treatment, etc.

2. Do not share things concerning your marriage that are of an intimate nature. In the lesson on the sexual relationship, you will gain much by discussing what the Scriptures say about physical union in marriage, right attitudes and how to have them, and steps you are taking to renew your mind. These types of things will be very helpful to discuss, and a wonderful dialogue about the sexual relationship can be had without sharing things that are personal to you and your beloved.

3. Remember, this study is to help YOU learn to be more like Jesus Christ and a *creative counterpart* to your husband. Surely your husband needs to change, too, but trust God to work on your husband as *you* concentrate on what *you* should be before the Lord.

4. If you are in a group, do not wait until the night before the group meets to do your lesson. Get busy early in the week to allow ample time to apply the principles and projects to your life before you get together.

I pray that you will faithfully apply God's principles to your marriage relationship to that you might become a Creative Counterpart!

Sincerely in Christ,
Linda Dillow

The Beautiful Blueprint

Read Chapter 2 at least once.

During the study this week, you will be reading and answering questions about Proverb 31:10–31. Many times we do not really see and understand the Scriptures until the fifth or sixth reading! It will be helpful to read the passage in different translations. Read the New King James, The Amplified Bible, and The Living Bible paraphrase, for instance.

As you read the passage, look for characteristics of the excellent wife in six areas. Many verses will apply to more than one area. Additional Scripture references are listed after each section and you may refer to them if you like. (It is best to look these up on your own, rather than taking time from the group; and even though it will be time-consuming, looking them up will aid your understanding.)

1. Read Proverb 31:10–31 looking for all you can find about *her relationship with God.* (Matt. 6:33; Prov. 3:5,6; Ps. 37:3–5; Matt. 22:37,38.)

2. Read Proverb 31 again and list *her characteristics as a wife*. (Prov. 12:4; 18:22; 19:14; Eph. 5:33; 1 Pet. 3:1–6; Titus 2:4–5.)

3. Read Proverb 31 a third time. What do you see about *her as a mother*? (Ps. 127:3; Prov. 22:6; Deut. 6:4–9; Prov. 15:20; Eph. 6:1–4.)

4. Reading the passage again, look for all *her homemaking abilities*. (Titus 2:5; 1 Cor. 14:33; 1 Cor. 10:31; Isa. 32:18; Prov. 15:17; Ps. 101:2.)

5. Read Proverb 31 again. How did she stretch herself as a woman in the area of her *talents and interests*? Physically? Creatively? (Rom. 12:3–8; Matt. 19:19; Acts 18:1–3.)

6. Reading a sixth time, note how the virtuous wife reaches out to others. (2 Cor. 5:19,20; Phil. 4:3; Acts 9:36–39; Acts 18:26; Heb. 13:2.)

7. In Proverbs 3:15; 8:11, and 20:15, we are told to value godly wisdom above jewels. How do you think these passages relate to Proverbs 31:10 and 31:30?

MAKING GOD'S WORD REAL TO ME

1. Considering the virtuous wife of Proverb 31 and all you have learned about her in these six areas, write your personal goal for this year for each of these areas. Be specific and try to use words that require action. (Illustration: c. Your relationship to the children— Spend one hour a week alone with each child.)

   a.   Your relationship to God—

   b.   Your relationship to your husband—

   c.   Your relationship to the children—

    d. Your homemaking abilities—

    e. Yourself as a woman—

    f. Your outreach to others (through outside activities)—

2. This week find time to be alone with God and talk to Him about this beautiful example of womanhood in Proverbs—and about YOU! Pray along these lines:

    a. Thank God for the beautiful blueprint in Proverb 31.

    b. Thank Him for what He wants to do in your life in making you a *creative counterpart.*

    c. Pour out your heart to Him and tell Him all your fears, lacks, and inadequacies as you view the woman in Proverb 31.

    d. Ask Him to begin working in your life to move you toward your goals.

    e. Thank Him for His faithfulness!

    f. Choose one verse from Proverb 31 to memorize and claim in your life. You may want to choose verse 30 or verse 10. Select the verse that speaks to you personally. Write it here and commit it to memory.

God's Game Plan

Read Chapter 3 at least once.

1. Incorrect views of the Christian life:

I *Must Do It All* (The Guilt Trip)	God *Does It All* (The Mystical Takeover)
a. Read Romans 7:14–20 b. Write an example from your life when you tried to "do it all."	a. Write an example from your life when you didn't do your part and wanted "God to do it all."

c. What were the results? | b. What were the results?

2. The Christian life is 100 percent God plus 100 percent us being in step with Him. Philippians 2:12,13 in *The Living Bible* says: ". . . And now that I am away, you must be even more careful to do the good things that result from being saved, obeying God with deep reverence, shrinking back from all that might displease him. For God is at work within you, helping you want to obey him, and then helping you do what he wants."

a. What does God ask us to do in our 100 percent according to these verses?

b. What does God promise to do in His 100 percent according to these verses?

GOD'S 100 PERCENT

GOD'S PAST PROVISION

3. God has given us a new position in Christ. Read 2 Corinthians 5:21 and answer these questions.

    a. What did we give to Christ? _____

    b. What did Christ give to us? _____

4. What happens when we become a new person in Christ? (2 Cor. 5:17.)

5. Who is our source of power and what does He promise to do? (John 14:16,17; John 14:25,26; John 16:7–14.)

6. Pick one: New Position, New Person, or New Power; express what this means to you experientially. (Illustration: New Position—God has placed me in Christ and because of my position I know God is not angry with me when I fail. This encourages me.) Of course, you can do all three if you like!

GOD'S PRESENT PROMISES

7. What is your major concern in your relationship with your husband right now?

8. Look up each verse listed below and record the promises you find. Then apply each promise to the situation you described in number 7. The first promise verse is done as an example.

Promise	Application
Heb. 13:5—I will never leave you or forsake you.	God will stand with me by my side as I try to accept my husband unconditionally.
Rom. 8:28,29	
Rom. 5:3–5	
1 Cor. 10:13	
1 Pet. 5:7	
Phil. 4:13	
Phil. 4:19	

MAN'S 100 PERCENT

9. God's 100 percent is to empower us through the
    Holy Spirit and to encourage, motivate, and guide
    us. Read 1 Corinthians 4:2 and record what man's
    part is.

We prove our faithfulness to God by trusting in
all God has done in the past and all He promises
to do for us daily. Secondly, we show that we
are faithful by *obeying* and taking steps to change
our attitudes and actions. It is a lifelong process
of growth to become like Jesus Christ, but God
wants us to get started, so how about this week!

Trust	Obey
1. This week commit the problem you listed under number 7 to God and claim His promises for you and your husband in this area from number 8.	1. Thank God that He is in control of the situation you mentioned in number seven.
	2. Ask Him to show you how you can obey Him this

2. Write out a commitment to God giving the situation to Him.

week through your attitudes.

3. List one specific attitude you will work on improving this week. Then list a specific time or situation where you can put it into practice.

The Priority Planner

Read Chapter 4 at least once.

If you are doing these lessons with a Bible study group, do not wait until the night before the group meets to do this one. The application takes all week (at least)!

"For the reverence and fear of God are basic to all wisdom. Knowing God results in every other kind of understanding. 'I, Wisdom, will make the *hours of your day more profitable* and the years of your life more fruitful'" (Prov. 9:10,11 TLB, italics added). Wisdom equals skill, skill in living life beautifully. We are told that by obtaining God's wisdom the hours of our day will be more profitable! Just what we all want and need!

This lesson concentrates on helping you "plan your priorities." In order to keep our priorities straight, we need skill. Our relationship with Jesus Christ must be our first priority.

1. When is the best time for you to have a devotional time with the Lord and how can you arrange it so you can have this time?

2. What does 1 Thessalonians 5:17 mean to you personally?

3. Why are we to pray? See Philippians 4:6,7.

4. What does God's Word do for us? See 2 Timothy 3:15–17, Psalm 119:11,105.

It is helpful to have a definite plan for your devotional time. In the back of this book is a daily Bible-reading plan. This simple plan will take you through the New

Testament twice a year and the Old Testament once if you read an average of four chapters a day! Begin *today* with the reading for this date! (Don't be discouraged if today's lesson is in Judges; you will alternate between the Old and New Testaments).

5. Think for a moment about last week. Record below, as best as you can remember, the amount of time spent in each of your six priority areas. How much time did you spend with your husband last week? Think in terms of quality time, not just time spent in the house with him watching television and you folding clothes! Perhaps you could think in terms of special time. It will not add up to 100 percent, as you spend a lot of time sleeping! This is a general evaluation that will help you see if your priorities are in order.

(1.) Special time spent with the Lord

(2.) Special time spent with my husband

(3.) Special time spent with the children

(4.) Special time spent on my home

(5.) Special time spent on me

(6.) Special time spent with those outside my home

Planning each week with your priorities before you *forces* you to think through how you are spending your time. It will be best to use the *Priority Planner* in doing this exercise but you can make a priority sheet following the format on pages 73 and 74 if you do not have one yet.

1. List one special thing to do under each of the six priorities.
   Illustration: Husband—go on a date *alone*.
   Lord—read my four chapters a day this week.

2. Now transfer the special project under each priority to the appropriate place on the weekly schedule.
   Illustration: Date with husband is Tuesday.

3. Then fill in the major things to do that week on the weekly schedule.
   Illustration: Friday—Bible Study, Tuesday—PTA meeting.

4. Make out your menus for the week with as little or as much detail as you personally need.

5. Now make out your shopping list being sure to list all the ingredients you need to fulfill your menus.

6. Write down on the daily schedule for tomorrow three to six things you want to accomplish. Each evening repeat this process for the next day.

NOW! Follow through daily with your "special projects" for this week and do what your Priority Planner says to do! God wants us to have goals—but don't get discouraged if all is not perfect the first week. PRAY, PLAN, and PERSEVERE! By faithfully planning your priorities you will be "numbering your days that you might gain a heart of wisdom."

My Own Robert Redford

Read Chapter 5 at least once.

God loves us unconditionally in Christ. When we have experienced His forgiveness and acceptance of us, we are more able to forgive and accept others—including our husbands!

1. Write a brief summary of how you received Jesus Christ as your personal Savior and Lord.

2. According to 1 John 5:11–13, what does the Christian possess?

3. Paraphrase Romans 8:35–39. What does this mean to you?

4. What does Christ promise to do for His sheep in John 10:27–30?

We can never be separated from God's unconditional love and acceptance. Now let's work on ridding ourselves of negative attitudes so we can accept our husbands as God accepts us! You will need separate sheets of paper to do the following exercises as they are just for you and the Lord.

5. Turn to page 96 in this book and read the instructions under Step 2. (Get rid of the plank in your own eye.) Take a separate sheet of paper and make a chart like the chart on page 98. Write down your husband's faults in the left column and your wrong responses in the right. After you have finished, confess your wrong attitudes to God and burn the paper.

6. Look at the chart on page 101 of this book. On another sheet of paper, copy down the two headings: Category of Expectation on the left and Desired Change ("My Rights") on the right. Next, write down the nine Categories of Expectation (Personal Habits, Children, etc.) Then fill in what you have wanted changed in each area. (If all the areas do not apply to you just do the ones that do.) When you have finished, write Philippians 2:5–7 across the chart and give up your rights to everything you think you deserve in a husband. Then throw the chart away.

Now we are ready to begin with the positive!

7. Look up and paraphrase Philippians 4:8. What does this mean to you in relationship with your husband?

8. Write a list of everything positive about your husband. There is a big space to write, so tell it all!

9.   Write out your commitment to God of your accep-
     tance of your husband.

His Greatest Fan

Read Chapter 6 at least once.

1. Look up Ephesians 5:33 (in more than one version if possible) and then write your own definition of reverence.

2. Fill in this chart, giving examples of when you have built your husband up in public and in private, and when you have torn him down. Give the results, too!

In Public	In Private
Built him up	

Results	
Torn him down	
Results	

3. These questions are designed to help you discover more about your husband. Write down your answers and then, when you and your husband

are alone, ask him *his* answers. Then, give him a list of these questions and let him answer them about you!

(1) What is the happiest thing that has ever happened to your husband?

(2) What has been the hardest experience of his life?

(3) What are his secret ambitions, the goals in his life?

(4) What are his deep fears?

(5) What traits of yours would he like to see changed?

(6) What does he appreciate about you the most?

(7) What man or men does he most admire?

4. What are your husband's interests and hobbies? How can you become more involved in them?

5. James 1:19 says, "Dear brothers, don't ever forget that it is best to listen much, speak little and not become angry" (TLB). How can you be a better listener with your husband this week?

6. List here qualities your husband has in these four areas:

Physical	Emotional
Spiritual	Mental

7. Pick one specific thing from each of the above four areas: spiritual, physical, mental, and emotional. Write the four you choose here. Ask God to show you a time and a way this week to admire your husband for each of the four. Remember, though, to do your 100 percent to look for a time and a way!

(1.) Physical—

(2.) Emotional—

(3.) Spiritual—

(4.) Mental—

The Executive Vice President

Read Chapters 7 and 8 at least once.

1. What does Ephesians 5:21 say to you personally?

2. Read and study carefully Ephesians 5:21–33. Fill in the two columns below with all you find in this passage concerning the man's role and the woman's role.

Wife's Role	Husband's Role

3. Ask your husband what it means to *him* for a wife to be submissive. Also ask him how you can be a more submissive wife and record his answer here.

4. Summarize 1 Peter 2:18–3:9 in your words.

5. What does this passage in 1 Peter 2 and 3 say to you as a wife?

6. Relate a situation in your marriage when you returned an insult for an insult. What were the results?

7. Describe a situation in your marriage when you returned a blessing for an insult. What were the results?

8. Put into words your desire to be a submissive wife, a wife who returns a blessing that she might inherit a blessing.

The Creative Lover

Read Chapters 9 and 10 at least once.

1. What does 1 Corinthians 7:3,4 say to you?

2. Read Proverb 5:15,18,19 in several translations of the Bible and write your own paraphrase of these verses. How do these verses relate to the context of Proverb 5?

3. What does Paul mean in Ephesians 5:31,32 that the two being one are a picture of Christ and His church?

4. How does Ephesians 5:33 relate to Ephesians 5:31,32?

5. Read the Song of Solomon in one sitting. (It's only eight short chapters, so take heart!) After reading the Song and the other verses above, write a paragraph describing how you think God views the physical dimension of your marriage.

6. Reread the steps to overcoming inhibitions on pages 187–191 of this book.

a. Renew your mind. You have been doing this in this lesson as you've read the Scriptures. Continue to read God's Word and choose one of these books to read (or perhaps another one you know about) on your sexual relationship this month! (*The Act of Marriage* by Tim and Beverly LaHaye, *Solomon on Sex* by Joseph Dillow, or *Love Life for Every Married Couple* by Gaye and Ed Wheat). The name of the book you will read is _____

_____ .

b. Memorize and meditate on God's Word. Choose one verse from this list concerning your sexual relationship to memorize this week: 1 Corinthians 7:4; Proverb 5:18,19; Song of Solomon 5:16. My verse for this week is _____.

c. Decide with your *will* to be God's version of a creative lover.

d. Do your part—your 100 percent! Decide what your part can be *this* week. Is it being totally available, aggressive, creative, or something else?

e. Give God time to work! He will be faithful to do His 100 percent as you do your 100 percent.

7. If you like you can list one creative thing you will do in the area of your sexual relationship within the next month. My creative project will be:

The Consistent Responder

Read Chapter 11 at least once.

1. Tell about a circumstance in your life that caused you frustration. How should you have responded to the situation?

2. According to 1 Thessalonians 5:18, what does God want you to do if there is a circumstance in your life now that is causing you anxiety? Write out a "thank you" to God for the circumstance that is troubling you now. Remember that giving thanks involves your *will* and adopting God's viewpoint concerning the problem.

3. Paraphrase Philippians 4:11–13, personalizing it to your own situation. (Illustration: "I have learned to be content with tiredness and dirty diapers. . . .")

4. What are your choices when your husband does not respond as you would like him to?

5. According to 1 Peter 3:9, how should you respond when you are hurt?

6. God has forgiven you in Jesus Christ and wants
   you to forgive yourself when you fail. What does
   God say about your sin in the following passages?

   a. Proverb 28:13

   b. Isaiah 38:17

   c. Isaiah 43:25

   d. Psalm 103:11,13

   e. 1 John 1:9

   f. Hebrews 8:12

If God does not remember your sin, then you need to
follow in His footsteps and put your sin behind you.
When you fail, ask God's forgiveness, and then forgive
yourself and move forward!

List the three areas discussed in this book where you feel the *most* competent.	List the three areas discussed in this book where you feel the *least* competent.
1.	1.
2.	2.
3.	3.

Now take number one where you feel the least competent and put it down for this month. Then take number two and put it on the calendar for next month. Continue listing areas until the entire calendar is filled!

January

February

March

April

May

June

July

August

September

October

November

December

It is exciting to be on the road headed toward the goal of being a *creative counterpart*. God will always be faithful to do His 100 percent through the Holy Spirit as you diligently do yours!

Planned Daily Bible Reading

By Professor J. Elwood Evans
Dallas Theological Seminary

This simple plan for daily Bible reading will take you through the New Testament twice a year and the Old Testament once a year if you read an average of two chapters each morning and two chapters each evening. The Old and New Testament books are interspersed to increase interest. The Old Testament books are read in order historically while the New Testament books are grouped by subject matter. The time from December 12 to December 31 can be used to catch up on any readings missed during the year.

Circa* 10,000–2,000 B.C.

  Jan. 1—Gen. 1–3
  Jan. 2—Gen. 4–6
  Jan. 3—Gen. 7–11

Patriarchal Times

  Jan. 4—Job 1–4
  Jan. 5—Job 5–8
  Jan. 6—Job 9–12

  Jan. 7—Job 13–16
  Jan. 8—Job 17–20
  Jan. 9—Job 21–24
  Jan. 10—Job 25–28
  Jan. 11—Job 29–32
  Jan. 12—Job 33–37
  Jan. 13—Job 38–42

Designed for Jews

  Jan. 14—Matt. 1–4
  Jan. 15—Matt. 5–8

* Approximately; about.

Jan. 16—Matt. 9–12
Jan. 17—Matt. 13–16
Jan. 18—Matt. 17–20
Jan. 19—Matt. 21–24
Jan. 20—Matt. 25–28

Jewish Christian Epistles

Jan. 21—James 1–5
Jan. 22—Heb. 1–4
Jan. 23—Heb. 5–8
Jan. 24—Heb. 9–13

Circa 1,950–1,600 B.C.

Jan. 25—Gen. 12–15
Jan. 26—Gen. 16–19
Jan. 27—Gen. 20–23
Jan. 28—Gen. 24–27
Jan. 29—Gen. 28–31
Jan. 30—Gen. 32–35
Jan. 31—Gen. 36–40
Feb. 1—Gen. 41–45
Feb. 2—Gen. 46–50

Jewish Christian Epistles

Feb. 3—1 Pet. 1–5
Feb. 4—2 Pet. 1–3, Jude

Circa 1,520–1,441 B.C.

Feb. 5—Exod. 1–4
Feb. 6—Exod. 5–8
Feb. 7—Exod. 9–12
Feb. 8—Exod. 13–16
Feb. 9—Exod. 17–20
Feb. 10—Exod. 21–24
Feb. 11—Exod. 25–28
Feb. 12—Exod. 29–32
Feb. 13—Exod. 33–36
Feb. 14—Exod. 37–40
Feb. 15—Lev. 1–3
Feb. 16—Lev. 4–7
Feb. 17—Lev. 8–11
Feb. 18—Lev. 12–15
Feb. 19—Lev. 16–19
Feb. 20—Lev. 20–24
Feb. 21—Lev. 25–27

Designed for Romans

Feb. 22—Mark 1–4
Feb. 23—Mark 5–8
Feb. 24—Mark 9–12
Feb. 25—Mark 13–16

Circa 1,441–1,401 B.C.

Feb. 26—Num. 1–9
Feb. 27—Num. 10–18
Feb. 28—Num. 19–27
Mar. 1—Num. 28–36
Mar. 2—Deut. 1–4
Mar. 3—Deut. 5–8
Mar. 4—Deut. 9–12
Mar. 5—Deut. 13–16
Mar. 6—Deut. 17–20
Mar. 7—Deut. 21–24
Mar. 8—Deut. 25–29
Mar. 9—Deut. 30–34

Concerning Christ's Return

Mar. 10—1 Thess. 1–5
Mar. 11—2 Thess. 1–3

Circa 1,401–1,375 B.C.

Mar. 12—Josh. 1–4
Mar. 13—Josh. 5–8
Mar. 14—Josh. 9–12
Mar. 15—Josh. 13–16
Mar. 16—Josh. 17–20
Mar. 17—Josh. 21–24

Circa 1,375–1,075 B.C.

Mar. 18—Judg. 1–4
Mar. 19—Judg. 5–7
Mar. 20—Judg. 8–12
Mar. 21—Judg. 13–16
Mar. 22—Judg. 17–21
Mar. 23—Ruth 1–4

Concerning Justification by Faith

Mar. 24—1 Cor. 1–4
Mar. 25—1 Cor. 5–8
Mar. 26—1 Cor. 9–12

Mar. 27—1 Cor. 13–16
Mar. 28—2 Cor. 1–4
Mar. 29—2 Cor. 5–8
Mar. 30—2 Cor. 9–13
Mar. 31—Gal. 1–6
April 1—Rom. 1–4
April 2—Rom. 5–8
April 3—Rom. 9–12
April 4—Rom. 13–16

Circa 1,065–965 B.C.

April 5—1 Sam. 1–3
April 6—1 Sam. 4–7
April 7—1 Sam. 8–11
April 8—1 Sam. 12–15
April 9—1 Sam. 16–19
April 10—1 Sam. 20–23
April 11—1 Sam. 24–27
April 12—1 Sam. 28–31
April 13—2 Sam. 1–4
April 14—2 Sam. 5–8
April 15—2 Sam. 9–12
April 16—2 Sam. 13–16
April 17—2 Sam. 17–20
April 18—2 Sam. 21–24

Devotional Hymns

April 19—Ps.   1–4
April 20—Ps.   5–8
April 21—Ps.   9–12
April 22—Ps. 13–16
April 23—Ps. 17–20
April 24—Ps. 21–24
April 25—Ps. 25–28
April 26—Ps. 29–32
April 27—Ps. 33–36
April 28—Ps. 37–40
April 29—Ps. 41–44
April 30—Ps. 45–48
May 1—Ps. 49–52
May 2—Ps. 53–56
May 3—Ps. 57–60
May 4—Ps. 61–64
May 5—Ps. 65–68

May 6—Ps. 69–72
May 7—Ps. 73–76
May 8—Ps. 77–80
May 9—Ps. 81–84
May 10—Ps. 85–88
May 11—Ps. 89–92
May 12—Ps. 93–96
May 13—Ps. 97–100
May 14—Ps. 101–104
May 15—Ps. 105–108
May 16—Ps. 109–112
May 17—Ps. 113–116
May 18—Ps. 117–120
May 19—Ps. 121–124
May 20—Ps. 125–128
May 21—Ps. 129–132
May 22—Ps. 133–136
May 23—Ps. 137–140
May 24—Ps. 141–145
May 25—Ps. 145–150

Designed for Greeks

May 26—Luke 1–4
May 27—Luke 5–8
May 28—Luke 9–12
May 29—Luke 13–16
May 30—Luke 17–20
May 31—Luke 21–24

Expansion of the Christian Faith

June 1—Acts 1–4
June 2—Acts 5–8
June 3—Acts 9–12
June 4—Acts 13–16
June 5—Acts 17–20
June 6—Acts 21–24
June 7—Acts 25–28

Concerning the Person of Christ

June 8—Philem., Col. 1–4
June 9—Eph. 1–6
June 10—Phil. 1–4

Circa 965–925 B.C.

June 11—Prov. 1–6

June 12—Prov. 7–12
June 13—Prov. 13–18
June 14—Prov. 19–24
June 15—Prov. 25–31

Concerning Church Matters

June 18—1 Tim. 1–6
June 19—Titus 1–3
June 20—2 Tim. 1–4

John's Writings

June 21—John 1–4
June 22—John 5–8
June 23—John 9–12
June 24—John 13–16
June 25—John 17–21
June 26—1 John 1–5
June 27—2 John, 3 John,
              Rev. 1–5
June 28—Rev. 6–11
June 29—Rev. 12–16
June 30—Rev. 17–22

Circa 965–925 B.C.

July 1—Eccles. 1–4
July 2—Eccles. 5–8
July 3—Eccles. 9–12
July 4—Song of Sol. 1–4
July 5—Song of Sol. 5–8

Gospel of a King

July 6—Matt. 1–4
July 7—Matt. 5–8
July 8—Matt. 9–12
July 9—Matt. 13–16
July 10—Matt. 17–20
July 11—Matt. 21–24
July 12—Matt. 25–28

Circa 965–587 B.C.

July 13—1 Kings 1–4
July 14—1 Kings 5–8
July 15—1 Kings 9–12
July 16—1 Kings 13–17
July 17—1 Kings 18–22
July 18—2 Kings 1–4
July 19—2 Kings 5–8

July 20—2 Kings 9–12
July 21—2 Kings 13–16
July 22—2 Kings 17–20
July 23—2 Kings 21–25

Jewish Christian Epistles

July 24—James 1–5
July 25—Heb. 1–4
July 26—Heb. 5–8
July 27—Heb. 9–13

Early Prophets
(c. 848–715 B.C.)

July 28—Obad., Joel 1–3
July 29—Jonah 1–4
July 30—Amos 1–4
July 31—Amos 5–9
Aug. 1—Hos. 1–4
Aug. 2—Hos. 5–9
Aug. 3—Hos. 10–14

Jewish Christian Epistles

Aug. 4—1 Pet. 1–5
Aug. 5—2 Pet. 1–3, Jude

Five Pre-exilic Prophets
(c. 750–610 B.C.)

Aug. 6—Isa. 1–4
Aug. 7—Isa. 5–8
Aug. 8—Isa. 9–12
Aug. 9—Isa. 13–16
Aug. 10—Isa. 17–20
Aug. 11—Isa. 21–24
Aug. 12—Isa. 25–28
Aug. 13—Isa. 29–32
Aug. 14—Isa. 33–36
Aug. 15—Isa. 37–40
Aug. 16—Isa. 41–44
Aug. 17—Isa. 45–48
Aug. 18—Isa. 49–52
Aug. 19—Isa. 53–56
Aug. 20—Isa. 57–61
Aug. 21—Isa. 62–66
Aug. 22—Mic. 1–3
Aug. 23—Mic. 4–7
Aug. 24—Nah. 1–3

Aug. 25—Hab. 1–3
Aug. 26—Zeph. 1–3

Gospel of a Servant

Aug. 27—Mark 1–4
Aug. 28—Mark 5–8
Aug. 29—Mark 9–12
Aug. 30—Mark 13–16

Circa 1,004–538 B.C.

Aug. 31—1 Chron. 1–4
Sept. 1—1 Chron. 5–8
Sept. 2—1 Chron. 9–12
Sept. 3—1 Chron. 13–16
Sept. 4—1 Chron. 17–20
Sept. 5—1 Chron. 21–24
Sept. 6—1 Chron. 25–29
Sept. 7—2 Chron. 1–4
Sept. 8—2 Chron. 5–8
Sept. 9—2 Chron. 9–12
Sept. 10—2 Chron. 13–16
Sept. 11—2 Chron. 17–20
Sept. 12—2 Chron. 21–24
Sept. 13—2 Chron. 25–28
Sept. 14—2 Chron. 29–32
Sept. 15—2 Chron. 33–36

Correcting Prophetic Errors

Sept. 16—1 Thess. 1–5
Sept. 17—2 Thess. 1–3

Weeping Prophet
(c. 626–580 B.C.)

Sept. 18—Jer. 1–4
Sept. 19—Jer. 5–8
Sept. 20—Jer. 9–12
Sept. 21—Jer. 13–16
Sept. 22—Jer. 17–20
Sept. 23—Jer. 21–24
Sept. 24—Jer. 25–28
Sept. 25—Jer. 29–32
Sept. 26—Jer. 33–36
Sept. 27—Jer. 37–40
Sept. 28—Jer. 41–44
Sept. 29—Jer. 45–48
Sept. 30—Jer. 49–52

Against Judaizers

Oct. 1—1 Cor. 1–4
Oct. 2—1 Cor. 5–8
Oct. 3—1 Cor. 9–12
Oct. 4—1 Cor. 13–16
Oct. 5—2 Cor. 1–4
Oct. 6—2 Cor. 5–8
Oct. 7—2 Cor. 9–13
Oct. 8—Gal. 1–6
Oct. 9—Rom. 1–4
Oct. 10—Rom. 5–8
Oct. 11—Rom. 9–12
Oct. 12—Rom. 13–16

Babylonian Period
(c. 593–571 B.C.)

Oct. 13—Ezek. 1–3
Oct. 14—Ezek. 4–6
Oct. 15—Ezek. 7–9
Oct. 16—Ezek. 10–12
Oct. 17—Ezek. 13–15
Oct. 18—Ezek. 16–18
Oct. 19—Ezek. 19–21
Oct. 20—Ezek. 22–24
Oct. 21—Ezek. 25–28
Oct. 22—Ezek. 29–32
Oct. 23—Ezek. 33–36
Oct. 24—Ezek. 37–40
Oct. 25—Ezek. 41–44
Oct. 26—Ezek. 45–48
Oct. 27—Lam. 1–5

Gospel of the Perfect Man

Oct. 28—Luke 1–4
Oct. 29—Luke 5–8
Oct. 30—Luke 9–12
Oct. 31—Luke 13–16
Nov. 1—Luke 17–20
Nov. 2—Luke 21–24

Christianity's First Thirty Years

Nov. 3—Acts 1–3
Nov. 4—Acts 4–6
Nov. 5—Acts 7–9
Nov. 6—Acts 10–12

Nov. 7—Acts 13–16
Nov. 8—Acts 17–20
Nov. 9—Acts 21–24
Nov. 10—Acts 25–28

Babylonian Period
(c. 605–530 B.C.)

Nov. 11—Dan. 1–4
Nov. 12—Dan. 5–8
Nov. 13—Dan. 9–12

Against Errors of Christology

Nov. 14—Philem.; Col. 1–4
Nov. 15—Eph. 1–6
Nov. 16—Phil. 1–4

The Persian Period
(c. 541 B.C.)

Nov. 17—Ezra 1–6

(c. 485–465 B.C.)

Nov. 18—Esther 1–5
Nov. 19—Esther 6–10

(c. 465 B.C.)

Nov. 20—Ezra 7–10

Pastoral Epistles

Nov. 21—1 Tim. 1–6
Nov. 22—Titus 1–3
Nov. 23—2 Tim. 1–4

The Persian Period
(c. 446–434 B.C.)

Nov. 24—Neh. 1–7
Nov. 25—Neh. 8–13

The Persian Period
(c. 520–400 B.C.)

Nov. 26—Hag. 1–2;
      Zech. 1–4
Nov. 27—Zech. 5–9
Nov. 28—Zech. 10–14

John's Writings

Nov. 29—John 1–4
Nov. 30—John 5–9
Dec. 1—John 10–13
Dec. 2—John 14–17
Dec. 3—John 18–21
Dec. 4—2 John 1–5
Dec. 5—2 John; 3 John
Dec. 6—Rev. 1–3
Dec. 7—Rev. 4–6
Dec. 8—Rev. 7–9
Dec. 9—Rev. 10–12
Dec. 10—Rev. 13–15
Dec. 11—Rev. 16–18
Dec. 12—Rev. 19–22